# THE DIVINE PLAN

Michael Cohen

Once again, special thanks to
my wife Melanie Lotfali,
for enduring this creative process
and turning ideas into reality.

## ACKNOWLEDGEMENTS

Thank you to Robin Mirshahi, Saname Ahdieh,
and Graham Nicholson for proof reading.

Copyright © 2017 Michelangela

The Divine Plan
by Michael Cohen is licensed
under a Creative Commons
Attribution-NonCommercial-ShareAlike 4.0
International License.

Version 1.0

ISBN 978-0-9945817-6-1

www.michelangela.com.au

# INTRODUCTION

This is the second book in the **Reflections on Reality** series.

In the first book, *The Big Story*, the false dichotomy perceived between evolution and creation was challenged. It was identified that the existence of the universe and everything therein, has come into being through a gradual, evolutionary, and divinely-ordained process.

Building on the foundation laid in the first book of the series, *The Divine Plan* examines social and cultural maturation throughout history. The impetus provided by the Manifestations of God for this maturation is explored, as are the symptomatic disintegrative and integrative forces at play within society today. It describes the opportunities, unique to this period of human history, available to the individual and the collective, to develop latent capacities essential to the establishment of a divine civilization.

# THE DIVINE PLAN

| | |
|---|---|
| **MATURATION** | **7** |
| Manifestations of God | 9 |
| Progressive Revelation | 11 |
| Early Manifestations of God | 15 |
| Krishna | 17 |
| Abraham | 19 |
| Moses | 21 |
| Zoroaster | 23 |
| Buddha | 25 |
| Jesus | 29 |
| Muhammad | 31 |
| Báb and Bahá'u'lláh | 35 |
| | |
| **DISINTEGRATION** | **39** |
| Spiritual Winter | 41 |
| Competition & Adverserialism | 43 |
| Materialism & Consumerism | 47 |
| Individualism | 49 |
| Fragmented Understanding | 51 |
| Misuse of Power | 53 |

## INTEGRATION — 55

- Interconnection — 57
- Unity in Diversity — 61
- Transition to Oneness — 63
- Reconceptualizing Human Rights — 65
- Reconceptualizing Power & Authority — 69
- Reconceptualizing Justice — 73
- Reconceptualizing Knowledge Generation — 75
- Reconceptualizing Consultation — 79
- Reconceptualizing Scientific & Spiritual Enquiry — 83
- Reconceptualizing Religion — 87

## THE DIVINE PLAN — 91

- The Eternal Covenant — 93
- The Lesser Covenant — 95
- Universal House of Justice — 97
- The Lesser Peace & The Most Great Peace — 101
- Ruhi Institute — 103
- An Invitation — 107

*Michelangela* — 109

# MATURATION

Much of recorded history has focused on politics, war, conflict, domination, and control, as well as scientific and technological advances. Human history has been deeply shaped by self-interested behaviors for millennia, and extreme expressions of such behavior have often resulted in, and continue to result in truly horrific consequences.[1] However, the social and cultural maturation of humanity over the past 6,000 years is a story much richer and more multidimensional. It is a story of the unfoldment of human capacity to build relationships between individuals, communities and nations, characterized by truth, trustworthiness, compassion, cooperation and justice.

# Manifestations of God

The Manifestations of God reflect the attributes of the Divine into the human world. The guidance They bring causes spiritual and material progress. God is likened to the sun - the energy source of physical life on Earth. The Manifestations of God are like the rays of the sun. They bring the heat and light to earth (humanity) in a form that is accessible and not overwhelming. Each Manifestation of God is also like a Divine Physician for the Age in which He appears. He reiterates the eternal and unchanging message of God's love for humanity, and also provides the guidance or 'medicine' required for the ills of the given period of history in which He appears. The Manifestations of God can also be considered as Divine Educators Who foster material, human, and spiritual education; providing the animating force through which the arts and sciences of the world advance.

> We are creatures, to a great extent, of our environment. But there is one Being Who is not the product of His environment. This is the holy Personage Who appears among us as the Manifestation of God. He is outside of and free of custom, tradition, and environment. It is only by following Him that we too are released from the ways of our ancestors and can start a new way. He is reality — truth — and the truth makes us free.[2]

# Manifestations of God

### Cycle of Fulfillment

| | |
|---|---|
| Bahá'u'lláh | 1863 CE. The Glory of God |
| Báb | 1844 CE or 0 BE, approximately 200 years ago Start of Bahá'í calendar. The word Bàb means gate, the gateway to the Revelation of Bahá'u'lláh |

### Cycle of Prophesy

| | |
|---|---|
| Muhammad | 622 CE or 0 AH, approximately 1,400 years ago Start of Islamic Hijra calendar |
| Jesus | 0 CE, approximately 2,000 years ago Start of Christian calendar |
| Buddha | 560 BCE, approximately 2,600 years ago in India |
| Zoroaster | 1,000 BCE, approximately 3,000 years ago |
| Moses | 1390 BCE, approximately 3,400 years ago |
| Abraham | 1,800 BCE, approximately 3,800 years ago |
| Krishna | 3,200 BCE, approximately 5,200 years ago in India |
| Adam | 4,160 BCE, approximately 6,200 years ago |

**Example of year:** If the date is 20 march 2014 CE (Current Era) in the Christian calendar, then it is equivalent to 1434 AH (Hijra year) in the Islamic calendar and 170 BE (Bahá'í Era) in the Bahá'í calendar.

# Progressive Revelation

Approximately once every 500-1,000 years a Manifestation of God is sent to humanity to provide the next installment of Divine Revelation. Some of the more recent Manifestations include Adam, Krishna, Abraham, Moses, Zoroaster, Buddha, Christ, Muhammad, the Báb and Bahá'u'lláh. The periodic unfoldment of God's will to humanity is known as progressive Revelation.

Each dispensation of divine revelation is associated with a particular Manifestation of God, and a particular time and place. Human beings then refer to a given dispensation of Revelation by names associated with that particular Manifestation - such as Hinduism, Buddhism, Christianity and Islam. However, these distinctions have no absolute reality and are simply labels which human beings have attached to a particular dispensation within one eternal process of progressive Revelation. This can be likened to the naming of the days of the week - Monday, Tuesday, Wednesday - while the rising and setting sun is just one reality, irrespective of the name of the day. Human beings have come to refer to the Messengers of God and the dispensation of Revelation associated with each of Them, by various names, though the divine guidance comes from one source and constitutes just one reality.

> The ocean is one body of water but different parts of it have particular designation, Atlantic, Pacific, Mediterranean, Antarctic, etc. If we consider the names, there is differentiation, but the water, the ocean itself is one reality. Likewise the divine religions of the holy Manifestations of God are in reality one though in name and nomenclature they differ.[3]

Viewed through the lens of progressive Revelation, it becomes clear that there is little benefit in clinging to a name given to a particular dispensation. Though there is a need to label and classify elements of reality, the fragmentation that can result from this needs to be resisted.

GOD

 Baha'i

One Light
Many lamps

 Islam

 Christianity

God is One
All religions are one

Buddhism

Judaism

Hinduism

The revelation of Christ released the energy and impetus to create spiritual and material change for a particular period of humanity's history. After Him, Muhammad released a new infusion of divine energy which lead to further progress. More recently, the dispensation of divine guidance revealed through Bahá'u'lláh has infused humanity with the power to make significant scientific and spiritual advances commensurate with humanity's current stage of development. Attachment to a particular Manifestation or the religion associated with His dispensation can lead to fragmentation of the essential oneness of religion.

> Humankind must be a lover of the light no matter from what lantern it may appear. Humankind must be a lover of the rose no matter in what soil it may be growing. Humankind must be a seeker of the truth no matter from what source it comes.[4]

It is attachment to names that prevents recognition of the truth of progressive revelation. That is, the fragmented thinking that results from over emphasis on labels which should serve as references only, limits our ability to recognize that Revelation is one ongoing spiritual and material process, delivered in chapters appropriate to the maturity of humanity at a given time.

> From the seed of reality, religion has grown into a tree which has put forth leaves and branches, blossoms and fruit. After a time this tree has fallen into a condition of decay. The leaves and blossoms have withered and perished; the tree has become stricken and fruitless. It is not reasonable that man should hold to the old tree, claiming that its life forces are undiminished, its fruit unequalled, its existence eternal. The seed of reality must be sown again in human hearts in order that a new tree may grow therefrom and new divine fruits refresh the world.[5]

Sistine Chapel — Vatican City.

# Early Manifestations of God

The Manifestations of God have provided a link between the Creator and humanity since well before recorded history. The guidance They have brought has been in direct response to the gradual increase in capacity on the part of human beings to receive and understand it.

> All that I have revealed unto thee with the tongue of power, and have written for thee with the pen of might, hath been in accordance with thy capacity and understanding, not with My state and the melody of My voice.[6]

Approximately six thousand years ago a Manifestation of God known as Adam founded a cycle of human development known as the Prophetic Cycle. Periodically throughout that cycle Manifestations of God appeared on earth, the traces of which humanity still has some record of. These include Adam, Krishna, Abraham, Moses, Zoroaster, Buddha, Jesus, and Muhammad.

The ability to record experience, and the means to preserve documentation are relatively recent human capacities. Thus, authentic and accurate documents pertaining to many of the earlier stages of the Prophetic Cycle either never existed, or have been lost to posterity. This has contributed to diverse interpretations, and even manipulation, of the original messages.

The information and understanding humanity now has regarding the teachings of the Manifestations of the early stages of the Prophetic Cycle is therefore often a distortion of the original teachings and reflect changes and interpretations made by human beings over centuries. This can create an impression of irreconcilable differences among the messages of the Manifestations, whereas in essence they are all part of one coherent process. The process itself has as its purpose the spiritual and material progress of the human race.

Hindu ritual — Kubu, Bali.

# Krishna

Krishna was an Avatar (Manifestation of God) sent by Brahman (God or Absolute Reality) to teach Dharma (universal laws, right way of living, and moral framework) to humankind. He was born in Uttar Pradesh (India) in 3,200 BCE (approximately).

The Dharma delivered by Krishna and previous Avatars represents the path by which humanity returns to virtue - through beneficence, purity, detachment, faith, truth, peace, restraint, respect, joy, love, contentment, and righteousness. According to common current understandings of the teachings of Krishna, individuals can travel three main paths: the path of good deeds, the path of enlightenment, and the path of love and worship.

Due to the antiquity of Krishna, Krishna's exact teachings and their impact on the culture of His time are not known with certainty. However, in the Bhagavad Gita, there is a record of Krishna's reference to the Eternal Covenant:

> Whenever there is a decline in righteousness, O Bharat, and the rise of irreligion, it is then that I send forth My spirit. For the salvation of the good, the destruction of the evil-doers, and for firmly establishing righteousness, I manifest myself from age to age.[7]

Cenotaph (tomblike monument) of Abraham — Ibrahimi (Abraham) Mosque, Hebron, West Bank.

# Abraham

The next Manifestation of God in the Prophetic Cycle, of which record remains, was Abraham. Abraham's name in Hebrew means "Father of Numerous Nations". He was born in Babylon, Mesopotamia (modern day Iraq) in approximately 1,800 BCE. At that time in history the religion of the Sabaeans was widespread. The people of the time embraced polytheism and denied the oneness of God.

When Abraham began to teach monotheism in a polytheistic idol-worshipping society he was exiled from Babylon to the Holy Land (modern day Israel). His teachings emphasized morality, and the spiritual purpose of life. They contributed to advancements in education and social welfare through the establishment of related institutions. These advances benefited thousands of people.

Through Abraham, God promised to provide for His followers, and commanded them to follow His laws. The descendants of Abraham were tasked with disseminating the message of the oneness of God.

> I will make thy seed to multiply as the stars of heaven, and will give unto thy seed all these countries; and in thy seed shall all the nations of the earth be blessed.[8]

The writings of subsequent Manifestations of God, including Moses, Jesus, Mohammad, and Bahá'u'lláh, explicitly acknowledge Abraham's role in the eternal process of revealing divine guidance to humanity. In the Qur'an, Mohammad attributes the first construction of the Kaaba[9] in Mecca to Him and His son, Ishmael.

Jewish Confirmation — circa 1900.

# Moses

Approximately 400 years later, in Egypt, Moses was born. At the time of His birth in 1,390 BCE, the Pharaoh had ordered the murder of all newborn Hebrew males. Though Moses was a Hebrew, he survived because He was found by the daughter of the Pharaoh, and raised within her household.

Moses' mission as a Manifestation of God began when God addressed Him through the 'Burning Bush' on Mount Horeb. His main teachings are summarized in the Ten Commandments, Thou shalt: have no other gods before me; not make unto thee any graven image; not take the name of the Lord thy God in vain; remember the sabbath day, to keep it holy; honor thy father and thy mother; not kill; not commit adultery; not steal; not bear false witness against thy neighbor; and not covet.

These teachings were revealed to a people who had reached an extreme state of depravation. The impact of Moses' teachings included the promotion of individual and collective responsibility and empowerment. His teachings encouraged acceptance of a moral law that transcends earthly or secular law; the concept of equality before the law; the sanctity of life and the dignity of the human being; the role of individual conscience and the value of personal redemption; the role of collective conscience and social responsibility; peace as an objective; and love as the foundation of justice.

Like the followers of Abraham, the followers of Moses, the Jewish people, entered into a covenant with God whereby God promised to guide them, and they promised to obey God. In due time, God will send another Manifestation of God.

> The Lord thy god will raise up unto thee a Prophet from the midst of thee, of thy brethren, like unto me; unto him ye shall harken; … I will raise them up a Prophet from among their brethren, like unto thee, and will put my words in his mouth; and he shall speak unto them all that I shall command him.[10]

Zoroastrian Eternal Flame at the Fire Temple — Yazd, Iran.

# Zoroaster

The next Manifestation of God in the Prophetic Cycle, of which record remains, was Zoroaster. He was born in Iran, in approximately 1,000 BCE. It is believed that from an early age he trained for priesthood. At the age of 30 he experienced a revelation from a shining being who taught of Ahura Mazda (Wise Spirit) and the six emanations of the Creator: purpose, truth, dominion, devotion, wholeness, and immortality. His teachings were documented in two books titled Gathas and Avesta.[11]

He taught that human beings possess the gift and responsibility of free will; taught monotheism; encouraged simplicity and minimization of ceremony in spiritual practice; proposed freedom from mind-altering plant-based drugs in rituals; and taught the oneness of all human beings in contrary to the oppressive class distinctions of his time.[12]

In the Gathas, Zoroaster refers to the ongoing human struggle between truth and falsehood. Zoroaster emphasized the freedom of the individual to choose right or wrong, and individual responsibility for one's deeds as the means to increase the emanation of truth in the world, and move closer to the Creator.

Mandala from Tibetan Buddhism — Sakya school lineage.

# Buddha

Approximately 400 years after Zoroaster, in Lumbinī, Nepal, Siddhārtha Gautama was born. Known to posterity as the Buddha, Siddhārtha Gautama was an Avatar (Manifestation of God) whose title means 'The Awakened One'. This son of King Śuddhodana was born around 560 BCE and died 80 years later in Kushinagar, India. Wishing for his son to be a great king, Śuddhodana shielded Him from religious teachings and from knowledge of human suffering. However, at the age of 29 Siddhārtha left the palace to live with His subjects, striving to understand aging, sickness, and death. After six years of asceticism and meditation, His station as a Manifestation of God became evident.

Acknowledging His divine station and power Buddha states:

> In the Heavens above and on the Earth below, I alone am the World-Honored One. All that exists in the Three Worlds is suffering, but I will bring comfort.[13]

The core principles of Buddha's teachings are referred to as the Four Noble Truths and the Noble Eightfold Path.

The First Noble Truth informs that life in this mundane world with craving and clinging to impermanent states and things, is unsatisfactory and painful. The Second Noble Truth informs that craving and clinging to this material life perpetuates suffering and dissatisfaction. The Third Noble Truth informs that it is possible to stop craving and clinging, and the perpetuation of suffering and dissatisfaction. The Fourth Noble Truth informs that the path to stop craving and clinging is the Noble Eightfold Path.

The Noble Eightfold Path is used to develop insight into the true nature of phenomena (reality). It is a fundamental tool for the rational mind to promote a more loving, just, and peaceful world.

Buddhist monks — Thailand.

**Noble Eightfold Path**

WISDOM
    Right View              Viewing reality as it is, not just as it appears to be.
    Right Intention        Intention of renunciation, freedom, harmlessness.

ETHICAL CONDUCT
    Right Speech          Speaking in a truthful and non-hurtful way.
    Right Action           Acting in a non-harmful way.
    Right Livelihood      A non-harmful livelihood.

CONCENTRATION
    Right Effort            Making an effort to improve.
    Right Mindfulness    Awareness without craving or aversion.
    Right Concentration  Correct meditation or concentration.

At the time of the Buddha, society was undergoing profound social change with many people renouncing the Vedic teachings which had traditionally served as a guide for society. Buddhism slowly spread until in 268 BCE when the Mauryan emperor, Ashoka the Great, declared Buddhism to be the state-religion of India.

Similarly to other Manifestations of God, the Buddha speaks of the ongoing process of divine revelation known as the Eternal Covenant:

> I am not the first Buddha Who came upon this earth, nor shall I be the last. In due time, another Buddha will arise in the world, a Holy One, a supremely enlightened One ... knowing the universe, an Incomparable Leader of men... He will reveal to you the same eternal truths which I have taught you. He will preach to you His religion, glorious in its origin, glorious at the climax and glorious at the goal ... He will proclaim a religious life, wholly perfect and pure, such as I now proclaim.[14]

Orthodox priests during Timkat ceremony — Medhane Alem church, Addis Ababa, Ethiopia.

# Jesus

About 500 years after the death of Buddha, or 2000 years ago (0 CE), Jesus was born into a family from Nazareth, Palestine (modern day Israel). His teachings built on the foundation laid by the Manifestations of God before Him. His teachings are summarized in His instructions to His disciples just prior to His crucifixion:

> A new commandment I give unto you, That ye love one another; as I have loved you, that ye also love one another.[15]

The state religion of first-century Roman Palestine was Judaism. As the number of people who accepted Jesus as a Manifestation of God grew, throughout the second and third centuries CE, His followers experienced opposition and persecution. In 313 CE the Roman emperor Constantine "had a dream in which he saw the Cross and heard the words 'Beneath this sign you will be victorious'."[16] After victory he then decreed that Christians should no longer be persecuted.

The impact of Jesus' teachings on society has been extensive. They lay the foundation for the current understanding of human rights, they led to the establishment of orphanages, and hospices. They underpinned the distribution of resources to the poor. The teachings of Jesus contributed to the cessation of the practices of human sacrifice, slavery, polygamy, infanticide of female infants, and divorce.

As with the Manifestations of God that preceded Him, Jesus entered into a covenant with His followers. He promised that God would guide them and admonished them to uphold their part in the covenant by following God's law. He also informed of the Eternal Covenant, and promised that another Manifestation of God would come after Him:

> Nevertheless I tell you the truth; It is expedient for you that I go away: for if I go not away, the Comforter will not come unto you; but if I depart, I will send him unto you.[17]

> I have yet many things to say unto you, but ye cannot bear them now. Howbeit when he, the Spirit of Truth is come, he will guide you unto all truth…[18]

The Kaaba at al-Haram Mosque during the start of Hajj — Mecca, Saudi Arabia.

# Muhammad

The Prophet Muhammad was born in approximately 570 CE in Mecca, Saudi Arabia, approximately 600 years after the birth of Jesus. Muhammad died in 632 CE in Medina, Saudi Arabia. He is known as the Seal of the Prophets because He was the final Manifestation of God in the Prophetic Cycle which began with Adam.

Muhammad lived in the desert of Hijáz on the Arabian Peninsula where the Arabian tribes were at the lowest depths of savagery and barbarism. They lived lives of pillage and robbery, perpetually engaged in fighting and war, plundering each other's property, capturing women and children whom they would sell to strangers. Daughters were buried alive, women were chattel without rights.[19]

Through the power of the revelation of Muhammad, over decades and centuries, a complete transformation of society occurred. Muhammad's teachings promoted peace, respect for Christians and Jews, religious freedom, advances in the empowerment of women, limitations on polygamy, freedom from slavery, humility before God, and generosity.

Muhammad taught His followers to know and love God. A Muslim is one who follows the religion of Islám. Islám is the religion based upon the teachings of Muhammad. The word Islam means surrender to God's will, as well as obedience, peace and salvation.

The impact of Muhammad's revelation on the Arabian population and on a vast region extending into Europe over many centuries is well documented…

The Arabs, upon the conquest of Alexandria in 642 CE, gained access to all the science of ancient Egypt, Persia, and Greece. They systematically built upon the sciences of medicine, manufacture, textiles, agriculture, astronomy, chemistry, philosophy, and mathematics. For more than five centuries science and education flourished under the influence of Islám.

Persian astrolabe.

Scientists influenced by the teachings of Muhammad made significant advances in the use of curative drugs, the establishment of hospitals, and clinical observations of diseases. Key texts developed in the region came to serve as the authoritative medical texts throughout the Middle Ages in all the medical schools of Europe.[20]

Chemists developed formulae for making the three chief mineral acids used by the modern world — nitric acid, sulphuric acid and hydrochloric acid, and developed the arts of distillation, oxidation and crystallization. The water-mill and windmill were also invented. These sciences and technologies were adopted throughout Europe.

Astronomical, geographical and navigational knowledge was systematically documented and exploited during this era. As a result the earth's circumference was ascertained, and tables of latitude and longitude for navigation on the Atlantic Ocean were devised.

Mathematics was transformed as a result of Islamic scholarship, with the development of Arabic numerals, the decimal system currently in use, and algebra. The word algebra is Arabic: 'al gebr', meaning "a binding together".

Similarly the science of agriculture was significantly advanced as seed stock from all around the world was collected and disseminated. This had impact on agriculture and diet throughout Europe as exotic spices, fruits, vegetables and coffee became available across the continent.

In the centuries following the revelation of Muhammad, the clothing of European populations was transformed by the sophisticated, colorful fabrics of the Arab world under the influence of Islám.

The Muslims founded the first universities in the ninth century in Baghdad, Cairo, Fez, Cordova and other cities. This educational model eventually spread to Europe where universities were established in Bologna, Padna, Paris and Oxford. The texts used in Christian Europe were translated from those used in the Muslim world, which seeded the renaissance in Europe.

The Greatest Name Yá Bahá'u'l-Abhá (O Glory of the All-Glorious) — Baha'i House of Worship, Wilmette, Illinois, USA.

# Báb and Bahá'u'lláh

Siyyid 'Alí Muhammad Shírází, titled The Báb (The Gate), was born in 1819 CE in (modern day) Iran, and executed in 1850 at the age of 30. He was both an independent Manifestation of God in His own right, and the Herald of Baha'u'llah, Who was His contemporary. The Báb lived for only six years after He announced that He was a Manifestation of God. However, His teachings so inspired the population amongst whom they were spread, that within those few short years over 20,000 men, women, and children came to have such strong faith in His teachings about the dawning of a new age, that they preferred to be killed by their oppressors, rather than deny their beliefs.

Mirza Husayn Ali, titled Bahá'u'lláh, was born in 1817 CE in (modern day) Iran. He died in 1892 in (modern day) Israel. Bahá'u'lláh opened a new cycle in human history, fulfilling the prophecies and covenant of all the Manifestations Who had come before Them. This new cycle, the Cycle of Fulfillment, began in 1844 CE. Bahá'u'lláh promised that there would be further Manifestations of God to follow, and that the next One would be manifest after at least 1,000 years.

Bahá'u'lláh teaches that God, as an unknowable essence, is one, though that essence may be referred to by a variety of names (for example Yahweh, Allah, Brahma, the Creator, Divine Spirit). He states that this one creator has created all of humanity, in its beautiful diversity, out of love. Therefore, all human beings are members of one human family.

'Abdu'l-Bahá, son of Bahá'u'lláh. Centre of the Covenant 1892-1921 — New Hampshire, USA, 5 August 1912.

Bahá'u'lláh explains that in order for humanity to attain its destined stage of maturity, it will need to develop capacity to eliminate all forms of prejudice and ignorance; independently investigate truth; and understand that the solutions to economic problems are fundamentally spiritual in nature. Humanity will come to recognize the inseparability of scientific investigation and the knowledge of reality that comes from religious teachings. He envisions a world where universal peace is upheld by a just world government; education is both universal and compulsory; and the people of the world are united in communication through means of a universal auxiliary language.

At the time and place of revelation, these teachings were considered at best radical and highly controversial, and at worst heretical. Although they are now widely accepted, the attitudes, qualities, knowledge, skills, and spiritual insight required to move them from the realm of ideal to the realm of reality are still in the early stages of development, for Bahá'u'lláh's teachings on spiritual reality go far beyond enunciating key principles for social development. The ultimate impact of Bahá'u'lláh's revelation on the world today will be a complete transformation and reordering of society at the level of the individual, community, and institution:

> The world's equilibrium hath been upset through the vibrating influence of this most great, this new World Order. Mankind's ordered life hath been revolutionized through the agency of this unique, this wondrous System — the like of which mortal eyes have never witnessed.[21]

Nuclear weapon test by the United States military — Bikini Atoll, Micronesia, 25 July 1946.

# DISINTEGRATION

Each dispensation of divine revelation passes through a cycle of potency, comprised of spiritual phases which can be likened to the spiritual seasons of spring, summer, autumn and winter. Currently humanity is awakening from its spiritual winter and slowly transitioning into its spiritual spring. The transition from spiritual winter to spiritual spring is often a time of tribulation, when inevitable change and resistance thereto disrupt age-old understandings and ways of being. It is a time when integrative and disintegrative forces simultaneously impact on society and its institutions, destabilizing and at the same time building anew.

> Such simultaneous processes of rise and of fall, of integration and of disintegration, of order and chaos, with their continuous and reciprocal reactions on each other, are but aspects of a greater Plan, one and indivisible, whose Source is God, whose author is Bahá'u'lláh, the theatre of whose operations is the entire planet, and whose ultimate objectives are the unity of the human race and the peace of all mankind.[22]

# Spiritual Winter

Spiritual winter sets in when individuals, misguided by human-created institutions, consistently reject or corrupt the guidance of God. The power inherent in the Teachings of the Manifestations of God is then dissipated, which leads to degradation and abasement of the individual and society. The passage below graphically describes this state:

> A world, dimmed by the steadily dying-out light of religion, heaving with the explosive forces of a blind and triumphant nationalism; scorched with the fires of pitiless persecution, whether racial or religious; deluded by the false theories and doctrines that threaten to supplant the worship of God and the sanctification of His laws; enervated by a rampant and brutal materialism; disintegrating through the corrosive influence of moral and spiritual decadence; and enmeshed in the coils of economic anarchy and strife—such is the spectacle presented to men's eyes…[23]

The spiritual winter from which humanity is struggling to emerge is again eloquently portrayed in the following extract:

> … in different nations in different ways, the social consensus around ideals that have traditionally united and bound together a people is increasingly worn and spent. It can no longer offer a reliable defense against a variety of self-serving, intolerant, and toxic ideologies that feed upon discontent and resentment. With a conflicted world appearing every day less sure of itself, the proponents of these destructive doctrines grow bold and brazen. We recall the unequivocal verdict from the Supreme Pen: "They hasten forward to Hell Fire, and mistake it for light." Well-meaning leaders of nations and people of goodwill are left struggling to repair the fractures evident in society and powerless to prevent their spread. The effects of all this are not only to be seen in outright conflict or a collapse in order. In the distrust that pits neighbor against neighbor and severs family ties, in the antagonism of so much of what passes for social discourse, in the casualness with which appeals to ignoble human motivations are used to win power and pile up riches — in all these lie unmistakable signs that the moral force which sustains society has become gravely depleted.[24]

Each of the previous dispensations of divine guidance addressed the spiritual and social needs of the population of its respective historical period.

> These holy Manifestations have been as the coming of springtime in the world… For each spring is the time of a new creation…[25]

## Competition & Adverserialism

Conflict, competition, and adverserialism permeate modern societies, and are perceived to be inevitable and essential dynamics of society where individuals and groups pit themselves as adversaries against each other within a battle for supremacy. Partisan politics, legal systems, economic systems, educational systems, and even systems of recreation and leisure, enshrine contest in varying forms.

Partisan politics is inherently competitive. It is based on the presence of two or more parties who compete for power, where the qualities and approaches that increase the likelihood of election, are not necessarily the qualities and approaches that best contribute to the wellbeing of society. On given issues, parties adopt a particular stance and defend this position against attacks from parties who have adopted a different stance. This process polarizes complex issues, creates false dichotomies and reduces complexity into slogans or black and white statements; thus, limiting opportunity to explore complexity and truth, and identify and implement holistic solutions.

Western legal systems are similarly adversarial. Legal representatives choose a side for which they advocate, and gather 'evidence' to convince a third party of their position. Rather than fostering a quest for truth or an exploration of reality, the legal system pits two parties against each other who then compete to 'win' a court case. In such a system, skills in 'playing' the adversarial 'game' can be more important than sincerity or fact. "Truth-obscuring tactics - such as omitting relevant but potentially harmful information, advancing exaggerated or false representations, obfuscating and distorting evidence, and coaching witnesses"[26] flourish in an adversarial legal system.

The free market is also inherently adversarial. A system wherein generating maximum profit constitutes the highest value, even at the cost of wellbeing of the individual and society; and fosters extremes of wealth and poverty, both within and between nations. Workers "compete against other workers for wages and capitalists compete against other capitalists for profit."[27] The outcome of this is a world in a perpetual state of instability, which, in turn, fosters "political conflict, crime, terrorism and war."[28]

Current educational systems also have their foundations in adverserialism. For example, students are taught to compete for rankings, rather than cooperate, and the capacity to debate, rather than consult, is highly prized. The generation of knowledge within academia takes place in a competitive and self-serving environment that undermines the investigation of truth, though this and the sharing of knowledge, should be the entire impetus for academic processes.

> Whether in the form of the adversarial structure of civil government, the advocacy principle informing most of civil law, a glorification of the struggle between classes and other social groups, or the competitive spirit dominating so much of modern life, conflict is accepted as the mainspring of human interaction. It represents yet another expression in social organization of the materialistic interpretation of life that has progressively consolidated itself over the past two centuries.[29]

Competition and adverserialism undermine justice and equity within society, thus contributing to disintegration.

> In the absence of a spiritual centre to which all can turn, individual and collective life in the world is often plagued by conflict and contention. Centers of authority and power compete to expand their spheres of influence, and some strive to achieve as much dominance as possible. At best, a humanity organized in this way can aspire to put an end to war and tolerate differences. Taken to the worst extreme, a state of perpetual conflict can end in total disintegration.[30]

# Materialism & Consumerism

Materialism is defined as the "preoccupation with or emphasis on material objects, comforts, and considerations, with a disinterest in or rejection of spiritual, intellectual, or cultural values."[31] Coherent with this understanding is the philosophy of materialism, which informs that matter is the fundamental substance or reality, while spiritual phenomena and consciousness arise only from the interaction of matter[32] (neurons in the brain). Thus, materialism denies a foundation of spiritual reality and can lead to the conclusion that material possessions and physical comfort are more important than spiritual values.[33] This understanding of reality serves as the basis for consumerism - "a social and economic ideology that encourages the acquisition of goods and services in ever-increasing amounts".[34] Consumerism is then, in essence, a religion for those denying a greater spiritual purpose.

Materialism and consumerism place economic activity at the centre of human existence and perceive it to be the main driver of progress.[35] Viewed through this lens, all elements of individual and collective life are subordinated to, and derive their significance from their connection to economic activity. The result is a culture where the worldly, the sensual, the material and the concrete are exalted; rather than the divine, the spiritual and the transcendent.[36] Economic activity unregulated by spiritual principles eventually leads to exploitation and corruption.

This culture, which is aggressively propagated across the globe, promotes a denial of spiritual reality, thus oppressing individuals from the knowledge of God.

> What "oppression" is more grievous than that a soul seeking the truth, and wishing to attain unto the knowledge of God, should know not where to go for it and from whom to seek it?[37]

Materialism and consumerism target the senses and the ego, leading individuals away from the spiritual search for meaning, thus contributing to disintegration.

# Individualism

Individualism emphasizes the centrality of the individual. The interests of the individual take precedence over the state or any given social group. It is believed that external interference in the choices of the individual by other individuals or institutions should be minimized.

In practice, individualism contributes to the devaluing of the individual's relationship with family, community and the environment, and supports an overemphasis on self and a harmful sense of entitlement. This self-focus is then aggressively exploited by those promoting consumerism.

Ubiquitous propaganda encourages indulgence and self-gratification, supporting the belief that the rights and desires of the individual are inherently more valuable than those of communities or society as a whole.

The manipulation to which those influenced by individualism are vulnerable, is a state where community and relationships are reduced to mere "means through which individuals achieve personal satisfaction and advancement".[38]

Individualism undermines the essential relationships between family, community, and environment which exist within a larger context of inter-dependence, thus contributing to disintegration.

Mural on the Berlin Wall at the East Side Gallery.

# Fragmented Understanding

A fragmented understanding is characterized by an ability to see only part of an entity, denying the whole and the interconnection among other parts thereof. It arises from the lack of recognition of inter-dependence and inter-connection among all aspects of reality. It can contribute to a lack of coherence among fields of knowledge, as well as dichotomous thinking about body and mind, the spiritual and the material.

In order to make sense of reality, human beings break knowledge into manageable pieces. When these pieces come to be seen only in isolation, and never as part of the whole to which they inherently contribute, fragmentation occurs.

For example, science and religion can be regarded as two complementary systems of knowledge, two windows into one reality. When the relationship between science and religion is understood in a fragmented way, false dichotomies are generated. A perception arises that only one or the other can be true and an acceptance of one, requires the rejection of the other.

Similarly, the human being is comprised of both a material form and a spiritual essence. When these elements are understood in a fragmented way, the importance of one or the other, and the relationship between them can be denied.

When a Manifestation of God is accepted to the exclusion of all others, rather than as one in a series of Divine Messengers, the eternal process of divine revelation is perceived in a fragmented way. History has shown that this erroneous fragmented understanding of what is essentially one unified process, causes conflict.

Fragmented understanding contributes to disintegration.

Ebensee concentration camp prisoners — Austria, 1945.

# Misuse of Power

Power in its most basic sense can be defined as the "ability or capacity to do something or act in a particular way".[39] When power is used correctly it necessarily contributes to the betterment and wellbeing of society. From the family to the international arena, the current period of history is characterized by the misuse of power.

Domestic violence is a manifestation of the misuse of power and control within an intimate relationship. Child abuse similarly constitutes the misuse of power that adults naturally and rightfully have over children. The willful concealment and active denial by powerful individuals and institutions is a misuse of power; the harmful effects of lead in petrol, tobacco, carbon emissions, and fast food, constitute a misuse of power at the societal level. The forceful appropriation of land and destruction of culture by colonizers of the Aboriginal peoples of the earth is a manifestation of power misuse that has caused harm across generations and over many centuries.

Power and its misuse are not synonymous, but the misuse of power is one of the greatest contributors to the disintegration of society. Understanding of power is currently limited by the culture of contest described in the above section - *competition and adverserialism*. Within a culture of contest, power is perceived to be of two kinds: power against an equal opponent, or power over an unequal opponent.[40] In both cases a second party with power is regarded as an 'opponent' and in the latter situation, it is considered inevitable that the unequal balance of power will lead to the more powerful party dominating the less powerful party. Misuse of power becomes normalized and is perpetuated generation after generation due to an inability to recognize alternative choices and courses of action.

> The expenditure of enormous energy and vast amounts of resources in an attempt to bend truth to conform to personal desire is now a feature of many contemporary societies. The result is a culture that distorts nature and purpose, trapping human beings in pursuit of idle fancies and vain imaginings and turning them into pliable objects in the hands of the powerful.[41]

The misuse of power destroys trust and relationships, thus contributing to disintegration.

# INTEGRATION

As noted previously, humanity advances through spiritual cycles or seasons. The periods of transition from winter to spring are characterized by the disintegrative forces described previously. These transitions are equally informed by simultaneous integrative forces which are creating revolutionary changes both within society and in our vision for what is possible.

These integrative forces have their source in the "law of oneness", which has been articulated by Bahá'u'lláh:

> Through Him the light of unity hath shone forth above the horizon of the world, and the law of oneness hath been revealed amidst the nations…[42]

According to this law, humanity should be considered as one soul:

> If any man were to meditate on that which the Scriptures, sent down from the heaven of God's holy Will, have revealed, he would readily recognize that their purpose is that all men shall be regarded as one soul…[43]

An understanding of oneness impacts on key elements of interpersonal relationships, such as cooperation, reciprocity, loving kindness, compassion, and altruism. It also impacts on the structures of society and leads to a reconceptualization of such concepts as human rights, power and authority, justice, and knowledge generation.

The concept of Oneness is a foundational truth - it has a reality that is independent of the choices made by the individuals, communities and institutions of society. Its outward manifestation is a goal towards which humanity is maturing, and this outer manifestation is emerging gradually. When action is aligned with oneness, it acts as a spiritual force for integration.

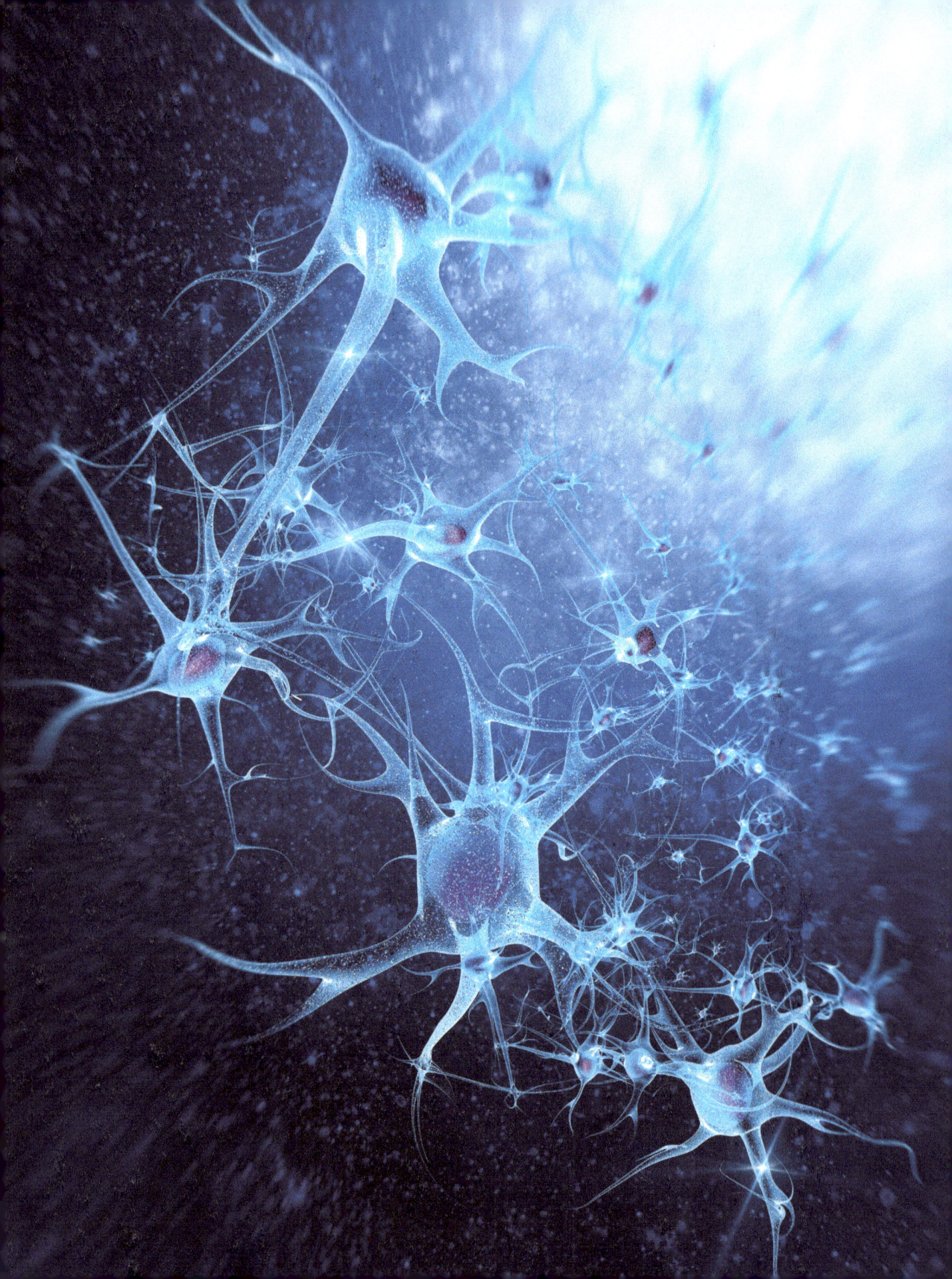

# Interconnection

As the outward manifestation of the oneness of humanity emerges, collective humanity is gradually taking-on an organic hierarchy. An example of organic hierarchy is found in the relationships among the cells, organs, and systems of the human body. This collective organic hierarchy will increasingly inform aspects of organization and coordination within the social organism. It will allow the diverse potentialities of every individual member to be realized in ways that contribute to the common good.[44]

Within this collective organic hierarchy no member will live apart from the whole, "whether in terms of contributing to its functioning or in terms of deriving its share from the well-being of the whole".[45]

> The individual cannot be understood in isolation from society any more than the cell can be understood in isolation from the larger body of which it is an organic part.[46]

Within this collective organic hierarchy there will be an equitable distribution of resources among individuals within the collective. Systems of resource distribution will empower rather than suppress the diverse members of the whole.[47]

> ...where the welfare of the part means the welfare of the whole, and the distress of the part brings distress to the whole.[48]

Playing its role within the collective organic hierarchy, each individual selflessly contributes talents and capacities for the betterment of the whole, just as each cell of the human body carries out its function and contributes to the wellbeing of the human organism.[49]

> Paradoxically, it is precisely the wholeness and complexity of the order constituting the human body - and the perfect integration into it of the body's cells - that permit the full realization of the distinctive capacities inherent in each of these component elements.[50]

Paenibacillus vortex bacterial colony.

Exactly how this collective organic hierarchy will ultimately manifest itself is unknown at this time, as the mature state of an organic entity cannot be comprehended by observing characteristics of its immature state.[51]

> As individuals enter into complex systems of social cooperation and reciprocity, individual consciousness itself is transformed. This, in turn, enables the emergence of still more complex systems of social cooperation and reciprocity which yields new collective capacities, and exerts a further transformative influence on individual consciousness, thereby releasing new and greater human potentialities.[52]

The power of oneness, as an emergent phenomenon, will manifest in society when the requisite level of integration and harmony are achieved among the diverse members of the social body.[53]

> It is precisely the diversity of the body's cells and organs that give rise to its emergent capacities.[54]

Woodburn Tulip Festival
Woodburn, Oregon, USA.

# Unity in Diversity

Recognition of the oneness of humanity does not promote uniformity. Whether at the level of biology or culture, diversity is essential to health and wellbeing, indeed to the very existence, of each individual and humanity as a whole.

In the words of Shoghi Effendi,

> It does not ignore, nor does it attempt to suppress, the diversity of ethnical origins, of climate, of history, of language and tradition, of thought and habit, that differentiate the peoples and nations of the world. It calls for a wider loyalty, for a larger aspiration than any that has animated the human race. It insists upon the subordination of national impulses and interests to the imperative claims of a unified world. It repudiates excessive centralization on one hand, and disclaims all attempts at uniformity on the other. Its watchword is unity in diversity such as 'Abdu'l-Bahá Himself has explained:[55]

> Consider the flowers of a garden. Though differing in kind, color, form and shape, yet, inasmuch as they are refreshed by the waters of one spring, revived by the breath of one wind, invigorated by the rays of one sun, this diversity increaseth their charm and addeth unto their beauty. How unpleasing to the eye if all the flowers and plants, the leaves and blossoms, the fruit, the branches and the trees of that garden were all of the same shape and color! Diversity of hues, form and shape enricheth and adorneth the garden, and heighteneth the effect thereof. In like manner, when divers shades of thought, temperament and character, are brought together under the power and influence of one central agency, the beauty and glory of human perfection will be revealed and made manifest. Naught but the celestial potency of the Word of God, which ruleth and transcendeth the realities of all things, is capable of harmonizing the divergent thoughts, sentiments, ideas and convictions of the children of men.[56]

> The well-being of mankind, its peace and security, are unattainable unless and until its unity is firmly established.[57]

Ceiling of the Sheikh-Lotf-Allah mosque — Isfahan, Iran.

# Transition to Oneness

When the oneness of humanity is truly embraced it will transform every aspect of all relationships, including relationships with self, family, community, institutions of society, and the natural environment. The move toward increased outer manifestations of oneness will be gradual, commensurate with the increased spiritual consciousness of individuals, and society as a whole.

> Spiritual consciousness can be understood in terms of our maturation from relative states of preoccupation with ego, self-interest, competition, and conflict, to states of altruism, selflessness, cooperation, and reciprocity. Similarly, this maturation process can also be understood in terms of an expanding awareness of our sphere of interconnectedness and interdependence.[58]

This transition to an increased revelation of the latent reality of the oneness of humanity, represents the final stage of a long evolutionary process in the collective life of humanity.

> The human species is an organic whole, the leading edge of the evolutionary process. That human consciousness necessarily operates through an infinite diversity of individual minds and motivations detracts in no way from its essential unity.[59]

It requires the reconceptualization of key elements such as self, culture, society, and humanity as a whole. Discourses underway in society are contributing to increased understanding of the concept of oneness and the implications of that foundational truth for the advancement of the material and spiritual aspects of society.

> Material civilization has reached an advanced plane, but now there is need of spiritual civilization. Material civilization alone will not satisfy; it cannot meet the conditions and requirements of the present age; its benefits are limited to the world of matter. There is no limitation to the spirit of man, for spirit in itself is progressive, and if the divine civilization be established, the spirit of man will advance.[60]

> Cooperation and reciprocity are essential properties which are inherent in the unified system of the world of existence, and without which the entire creation would be reduced to nothingness.[61]

Dove window at St Peter's Basilica — Vatican City.

# Reconceptualizing Human Rights

Human rights can be defined as:

> ...fundamental rights to which a person is inherently entitled simply because she or he is a human being, regardless of their nation, location, language, religion, ethnic origin or any other status. They are applicable everywhere and at every time in the sense of being universal, and they are egalitarian in the sense of being the same for everyone.[62]

The understanding and implementation of human rights is a maturing concept:

> The international human rights regime is the fruit of an ongoing process of moral dialogue among diverse nations and peoples. The human rights discourse provides a mechanism for people of divergent convictions to learn about each other, resolve particular disagreements, and arrive at new understandings of what is possible for human beings. This cross-cultural enterprise has gradually given rise to a new ethos of human solidarity and collective responsibility.[63]

The human rights discourse supports the liberation of oppressed individuals and groups through the application of justice. However, human rights founded on materialistic criteria alone are limited in their power to truly transform society.

> Without a transcendent basis for rights — a power that reaches to the heart of human consciousness and motivation — humanity will not be able to develop an integrated moral framework that will secure the advancement of all peoples. Without reference to the spiritual provenance, the protection of basic human freedoms cannot be guaranteed.[64]

This transcendent basis for human rights is founded on the concept of humans as spiritual beings, endowed with spiritual capacities, and brought to life to build a relationship with the Creator. The Bahá'í International Community comments:

Oblation statue by Guillermo Tolentino — University of the Philippines.

> The source of human rights is the endowment of qualities, virtues and powers which God has bestowed upon mankind without discrimination of sex, race, creed or nation. To fulfill the possibilities of this divine endowment is the purpose of existence.[65]

That is, the purpose of human existence is to know the source of spiritual reality and to align one's life with the guidance from that source.

> The first duty of the individual is the recognition of the Divine Authority that is the foundation of all law; the second is observance of that law. To exercise these twin duties may be regarded as the highest expression of free will with which every human being is endowed by an all-loving Creator. From this perspective, the right to exercise freedom of conscience in the matter of religious belief comes into being so that one can fulfill their spiritual duty of observing the commandments of God.[66]

> The innate and fundamental aspiration to investigate reality is thus not only the right but the obligation of every human being.[67]

Similarly the Universal House of Justice states:

> To accept the Prophet of God in His time and to abide by His bidding are the two essential, inseparable duties which each soul was created to fulfill. One exercises these twin duties by one's own choice, an act constituting the highest expression of the free will with which every human being has been endowed by an all-loving Creator.[68]

Human rights protect the liberty of individuals and groups within society. The most important liberty for any human being is the liberty to know and worship the Creator through knowledge of the Divine Manifestations. The ultimate purpose of human rights is to ensure this freedom for every human being.

> From a religious point of view, true liberty is compliance with divine teachings. For only to the extent that human beings awaken to a capacity for love, generosity, justice, compassion, trustworthiness, and humility can they manifest the extraordinary powers with which they have been endowed.[69]

The oneness of humanity will be realized when society universally acknowledges the human being as a spiritual being, created with the purpose to know and love the Creator. The redefinition of human rights framed by an understanding of spiritual reality will serve as an integrative force.

United Nations General Assembly Hall — New York City, USA.

## Reconceptualizing Power & Authority

Today, the prevailing understanding of individual power within society emphasizes the capacity to pursue one's self-interests, the capacity to compete against and dominate others, and the capacity to influence and manipulate. Yet individual power can also signify the capacity to work creatively and constructively with others in the pursuit of common interests; the capacity to empower, unify and transform; the capacity for justice and equity; the capacity for truth and trustworthiness; the capacity for empathy and compassion; the capacity for humility and detachment; and the capacity of altruism and self-sacrifice.[70] This alternate understanding of individual power is informed by recognition of the spiritual nobility of individuals.

The power to transform society lies in the Word of God. For this period of humanity's history, the Word of God constitutes the writings of the Manifestation of God for this age, Bahá'u'lláh. The power of truth, the power of unity, and the power of love, released through the Word of God will revive society. Collective thought and action will become increasingly aligned with the Will of God and the purpose of creation.

> Power can now be understood as a spiritual force that is infused into human relationships when they are organized and aligned in accordance with the underlying spiritual laws that govern reality.[71]

Partial view of the Mandelbrot set — step 7 of a zoom sequence.

The role of authority, in this context, is not to restrict human agency but to release it, by harmonizing and canalizing the creative powers that individuals and communities can draw upon in pursuit of global prosperity and well-being.[72]

> [Legitimate authority] can be understood as a capacity that is conferred by the social body on those whom it trusts to guide and coordinate its collective affairs, at appropriate levels of social organization, in pursuit of collective goals and aspirations.[73]

Within a spiritually mature society, power and authority cease to be instruments of dominance. They become necessary elements of social organization whereby certain institutions of society are invested with authority to promulgate spiritual laws, not to dictate but to create avenues through which human potential can properly unfold. Such a manifestation of authority gives rise to a spirit of loving, eager cooperation that binds individuals and their institutions in a most natural and loving way.[74]

> Power is not a finite entity which is to be "seized" and "jealously guarded"; it constitutes a limitless capacity to transform that resides in the human race as a body.[75]

The oneness of humanity will be realized from the understanding that true power occurs when individual and institutional relationships are aligned to spiritual laws. This alignment will contribute to integration.

Justice statue — Courthouse of Tehran.

# Reconceptualizing Justice

Justice is not simply determining right from wrong, being fair, or upholding morals; it is not merely the wish for those experiencing oppression; nor is it just the adherence to laws and regulations. Justice is an innate faculty of the human being which enables each person to distinguish truth from falsehood. Essentially, justice is characterized by the capacity to judge fairly and equitably, by seeing with our own eyes and not through the eyes of others. Justice is fair-mindedness wedded to an authentic search for truth.[76]

> The best beloved of all things in My sight is Justice; turn not away therefrom if thou desirest Me, and neglect it not that I may confide in thee. By its aid thou shalt see with thine own eyes and not through the eyes of others, and shalt know of thine own knowledge and not through the knowledge of thy neighbor.[77]

Justice animates the desire for service to humanity.

> The wellbeing of any individual or group can only be achieved by ensuring the wellbeing of the entire social body. Justice thus animates in us the desire and the will to exert ourselves for the betterment of all peoples.[78]

The purpose of justice is the appearance of unity among humankind.[79]

> Unity is the governing dynamic that underlies all of reality, even as justice is the only means by which this dynamic can find its full expression in our social reality.[80]

> Justice is the indispensable compass in collective decision making, because it is the only means by which unity of thought and action can be achieved.[81]

The oneness of humanity will be realized when society is ordered around an authentic conception of justice. Justice is the path to unity, and contributes to integration.

> …true oneness is only possible when society is organized around an authentic and adequate conception of justice. Therein lies the key to the transformative processes of individual and collective flourishing…[82]

Wikipedia monument — Słubice, Poland

# Reconceptualizing Knowledge Generation

There is a growing gap between the knowledge and theory generated by the privileged sectors of global society and the actual needs of the majority of human beings on this planet.[83]

> True learning is that which is conducive to the wellbeing of the world.[84]

There is also a pervasive pattern whereby the masses of humanity constitute passive recipients of knowledge generated by distant 'experts'. This expert and non-expert dichotomy disempowers the majority of the world's people to generate knowledge relevant to their needs. In order to address this, the innate intelligence, creativity, insight and innovation of all people must be recognized, and harnessed in the generation of knowledge.[85]

> Access to knowledge is the right of every human being, and participation in its generation, application and diffusion a responsibility that all must shoulder in the great enterprise of building a prosperous world civilization — each individual according to his or her talents and abilities.[86]

> The tasks entailed in the development of a global society call for levels of capacity far beyond anything the human race has so far been able to muster. Reaching these levels will require an enormous expansion in access to knowledge, on the part of individuals and social organizations alike. Universal education will be an indispensable contributor to this process of capacity building, but the effort will succeed only as human affairs are so reorganized as to enable both individuals and groups in every sector of society to acquire knowledge and apply it to the shaping of human affairs.[87]

Furthermore, the universal participation in the generation, dissemination and application of knowledge is not sufficient to foster integration when those processes are carried out within a materialistic framework. Revelation, or the guidance provided periodically from God to human beings, is essential to the generation of knowledge that is informed by, and accurately reflects reality.

Wikimania group photograph — 2012.

> The light which these [Manifestations of God] radiate is responsible for the progress of the world and the advancement of its peoples. They are like unto leaven which leaveneth the world of being, and constitute the animating force through which the arts and wonders of the world are made manifest.[88]

Revelation is the only source of foundational truths, or absolute statements about reality that are exalted above temporal, spatial, and cultural particulars or limitations. The Word of God provides guidance based on an accurate and unbiased understanding of all of creation, as well as of all the individual elements thereof.

Though Revelation is perfect, human understanding of it is imperfect. Human beings can only strive, over time, to gain greater insights, and apply with greater fidelity, this divine knowledge. This is achieved through an iterative and concurrent process of study, consultation, action, and reflection.

The oneness of humanity will be realized when universal participation in knowledge generation and dissemination is embraced within an interactive process to empower the masses of humanity. This empowerment will be an integrative force.

# Reconceptualizing Consultation

The decision-making processes of society are often characterized by adverserialism. As previously discussed, whether within politics, the legal system, academia, the media, or scientific investigation the processes of advancing knowledge and making decisions involve pitting people, groups or ideas against one another. However these adversarial processes often lead to the subtleties of reality, the truth, remaining concealed.

> Parliamentary procedure should have for its object the attainment of the light of truth upon questions presented and not furnish a battleground for opposition and self-opinion. Antagonism and contradiction are unfortunate and always destructive to truth.[89]

An alternative to adversarial decision-making is consultation which, when practiced faithfully, becomes an enquiry into truth.

> No power can exist except through unity. No welfare and no well-being can be attained except through consultation.[90]

The practice of true consultation assumes that the comprehension of any given individual is limited in relation to complex and multifaceted issues. Consultation then, draws on the benefit and contribution of diverse perspectives, facilitating all participants to reach greater depths and embrace increased complexity.[91]

> The heaven of divine wisdom is illumined with the two luminaries of consultation and compassion. Take ye counsel together in all matters, inasmuch as consultation is the lamp of guidance which leads the way, and is the bestower of understanding.[92]

The purpose of consultation is to seek truth through unity; thus, ideas presented during consultation are not owned by any individual. All ideas are tabled for consideration and are not referenced as ideas belonging to any one individual. Individuals strive to transcend their respective points of view in the search for truth.

> Man should weigh his opinions with the utmost serenity, calmness and composure. Before expressing his own views she should carefully consider the views already advanced by others. If he finds that a previously expressed opinion is more true and worthy, he should accept it immediately and not willfully hold to an opinion of his own.[93]

Maintaining harmony and unity throughout consultation is essential for successful consultation. Thus, the effectiveness of consultation is dependent upon the development of certain personal qualities by the participants in the process. These spiritual qualities include purity of motive, humility, truthfulness, fair-mindedness, loving-kindness, patience, impartiality, and detachment.[94]

> The prime requisites for them that take counsel together are purity of motive, radiance of spirit, detachment from all else save God, attraction to His Divine Fragrances, humility and lowliness amongst His loved ones, patience and long-suffering in difficulties and servitude to His exalted Threshold. Should they be graciously aided to acquire these attributes, victory from the unseen Kingdom of Bahá shall be vouchsafed to them.[95]

> The first duty of the members is to effect their own unity and harmony, in order to obtain good results. If there be no unity, or the committee becomes the cause of inharmony, undoubtably, it is better that it does not exist…[96]

Acknowledgement of the source of oneness, the Creator, assists participants to align their intentions to seek the truth and moderate their conduct with humility.

> [people must] turn their faces to the Kingdom on High and ask aid from the Realm of Glory. They must then proceed with the utmost love and devotion, courtesy, dignity, care and moderation to express their views. They must in every matter search out the truth.[97]

The effects of this method of consultation, by successively revealing ever-deeper truths about reality and the expression of the Creator in the material world, has profound impacts.

> If a small number of people gather lovingly together, with absolute purity and sanctity, with their hearts free of the world, experiencing the emotions of the Kingdom and the powerful magnetic forces of the Divine, and being as one in their happy fellowship, that gathering will exert its influence over all the earth.[98]

The oneness of humanity will be realized when consultation is centered around the investigation of truth, and where participants embody humility and detachment. The practice of true consultation with qualities of the spirit is an integrative force.

Body of Knowledge sculpture by Jaume Plensa — Goethe University, Frankfurt, Germany.

# Reconceptualizing Scientific & Spiritual Enquiry

> Throughout recorded history, human consciousness has always depended upon two basic knowledge systems through which its potentialities have progressively been expressed: science and religion. Through these two agencies, humanity's experience has been organized, its environment interpreted, its latent powers explored, and its moral and intellectual life disciplined. They have acted as the real progenitors of civilization, especially when working in concert.[99]

In order to frame its questions and articulate discoveries about material reality, science has developed, and continues to develop suitable language. Throughout history, as science has pushed frontiers of learning, the development of language to express emerging concepts has posed challenges. The shift from Newtonian physics to quantum physics, for example, was challenged by the differences in language and concepts required to articulate elements of the two frameworks. This challenge of developing language suitable for articulating the processes and outcomes of scientific enquiry, is ongoing. It is, however, embraced as part of the process of advancing science.

> …[thousands of years ago] humanity sought explanations for natural phenomena in magic and the arbitrary acts of gods.[100] [scientific theories] would have appeared quite radical and they could not have been empirically verified. Yet they must have appealed, intuitively, to a growing number of people who, consciously or unconsciously, committed themselves…[and] advanced the enterprise of science. Only with the passage of time has confidence grown regarding the premises underlying scientific enterprise…[101]

In order to learn about spiritual reality, an evolving set of concepts, and corresponding language suitable for the exploration of intangible dimensions of human existence, is required.[102] Metaphors and analogies must be relied upon to convey information about spiritual reality, to facilitate understanding of the intangible through reference to the tangible.[103]

> Just as human intellects have revealed the secrets of matter and have brought forth from the realm of the invisible the mysteries of nature, may minds and spirits, likewise, come into the knowledge of the verities of God, and the realities of the Kingdom be made manifest in human hearts.[104]

The language through which spiritual truth is expressed, like scientific language, strives to be objective. However it also draws on poetry, imagery, stories and parables, to convey meaning and to speak directly to the human heart.[105]

> Ways of thinking about the spiritual dimension of existence are limited by the constraints of human language and by our inability to conceive of that which transcends our own consciousness.[106]

Although there are challenges in expressing spiritual truth, it is becoming ever more apparent that this enquiry into spiritual reality is an essential aspect of humanity's collective maturity.

> Just because something is difficult to conceptualize and communicate with precision does not mean that it is not real, or that we should not seek to communicate about it more coherently over time.[107]

Both science and religion rely on faculties of the human soul. These faculties include…

> …reason, intuition, imagination, abstraction, attraction to beauty, truth, the ability to create models of reality, and the ability to remain detached from preconceived ideas. Both systems are collective endeavors, carried out by communities of imperfect people, and each system is thus enabled and constrained by the same complex social forces that characterize all collective human endeavors.[108]

> Both systems can and must be systematic, consultative, and reflective in their generation of knowledge. Both systems advance within evolving frameworks of knowledge that must become increasingly coherent over time as they are tested against reality.[109]

The challenge for humanity today is to engage in an ongoing and intensifying dialogue between science and religion. In every sphere of human activity and at every level, the insights and skills that represent scientific accomplishment must look to the force of spiritual commitment and moral principle to ensure their appropriate application.[110]

> Thus science - via practices such as empirical observation, induction and deduction, experimentation, and so forth - can be understood as a system through which humanity explores and exerts its influence over the phenomenal world. Likewise, religion - via the study of Revelation and the practices that derive from it - can be understood as a system through which humanity renders that world meaningful and achieves consensus regarding the codes and principles that must organize and guide human affairs.[111]

The oneness of humanity will become realized when science and religion become complementary systems of knowledge and practice by which humanity can "gradually gain deeper insights into the governing dynamics of the reality that emanates from God, that which reflects God's Will and Purpose".[112] The enquiry into reality which views both science and religion as windows viewing the same reality will act as an integrative force.

St Andrew's Catholic Church
— Roanoke, Virginia, USA.

# Reconceptualizing Religion

Religion is commonly understood as "a cultural system of behaviors and practices, world views, sacred texts, holy places, ethics, and societal organization..."[113] With this understanding, religion is perceived as something lacking in any power or reality beyond the psychological impact on the individual or community of believers.

In contrast, Bahá'u'lláh explains that religion is the living link between the infinite Creator and the finite creation. Like the rays of the sun bringing the energy of the sun to the earth in a manageable form, religion is the guidance from God to humanity in an accessible form. Its purpose is to allow the material and spiritual advancement of humanity.

> Religion, moreover, is not a series of beliefs, a set of customs; religion is the teachings of the Lord God, teachings which constitute the very life of humankind, which urge high thoughts upon the mind, refine the character, and lay the groundwork for man's everlasting honor.[114]

> [Religion], when it has been faithful to the spirit and example of the transcendent Figures who gave the world its great belief systems, has awakened in whole populations capacities to love, to forgive, to create, to dare greatly, to overcome prejudice, to sacrifice for the common good, and to discipline the impulses of the animal instinct. Unquestionably, the seminal force in the civilizing of human nature has been the influence of the succession of these Manifestations of the Divine that extends back to the dawn of recorded history.[115]

> The purpose of religion as revealed from the heaven of God's holy Will is to establish unity and concord amongst the peoples of the world; make it not the cause of dissension and strife. The religion of God and His divine law are the most potent instruments and the surest of all means for the dawning of the light of unity amongst men. The progress of the world, the development of nations, the tranquility of peoples, and the peace of all who dwell on earth are amongst the principles and ordinances of God.[116]

Throughout history, true religion has been inextricably intertwined with the maturation of civilization. It has served as the "the ultimate source of every praiseworthy aspiration, and the light that has illumined human understanding and enabled it to distinguish between the base and the noble."[117]

> The diseased condition of the body of humanity is attributable , in large part, to the neglect or corruption of religion as a unifying and civilizing social force; to the corresponding license that has been given to materialistic values, self-interested pursuits, and competitive impulses; and to the consequent formation of oppressive and exploitative social structures that are the cause of pervasive conflict and suffering in the world today.[118]

Religious revelation has been provided in successive chapters. The sacred texts of each dispensation of religion, are the books of Revelation - that which is revealed to humankind about spiritual and material reality. Obedience to the laws within those texts allows humanity to mature and prosper. Religion is the light of the world, and the progress, achievement, and happiness of man result from obedience to the laws set down in the Holy Books.[119]

> The methods of religion have fostered the development of spiritual perception, provided insights into the deepest questions of human purpose and existence, progressively clarified those shared values and essential principles that promote human well-being, bonded people together in ever-larger communities, and given constructive direction to individual and collective endeavors, including the enlightened application of scientific knowledge.[120]

Just as humanity is one, God's guidance to humanity is essentially one. That is, all religions are part of one unfolding Divine Plan.

> If Christians of all denominations and divisions should investigate reality, the foundations of Christ will unite them. No enmity or hatred will remain, for they will all be under the one guidance of reality itself. Likewise, in the wider field, if all the existing religious systems will turn away from ancestral imitations and investigate reality, seeking the real meanings of the Holy Books, they will unite and agree upon the same foundation, reality itself. As long as they follow counterfeit doctrines or imitations instead of reality, animosity and discord will exist and increase.[121]

The oneness of humanity will be realized when religious institutions acknowledge that all religions are part of one eternal process, with the purpose to establish unity and concord amongst the peoples of the world. When individuals align to an authentic concept of religion, it will act as an integrative force.

> Know thou that in every age and cycle, all laws and ordinances have been changed according to the requirements of the times, except the law of love which, like a fountain, ever flows, and whose course never suffers to change.[122]

The successive chapters of religion constitute a Divine Plan, an unfoldment of Divine Will as humanity gains increasing spiritual capacity. The current chapter of Divine Will, the Revelation of Bahá'u'lláh, has been unfolding within the modern world since 1844 CE.

> Religion, with the Word of God as its originating impulse, can be conceived as the ultimate "collective centre" around which the oneness of humanity can and will be achieved.[123]

# THE DIVINE PLAN

The Creator has provided guidance to humanity across the ages through Manifestations of God, some of Whom we know as Adam, Krishna, Abraham, Moses, Buddha, Jesus Christ, and Muhammad. The most recent Manifestations of God are known as the Báb and Bahá'u'lláh. As a result of the energy released into the world by Bahá'u'lláh, a twofold process has been set in motion. The disintegration of the elements of society that are not aligned with the Divine Plan; and the integrative processes that are contributing to the reconstruction of a new world order.

Symptoms of the disintegrative processes include an emphasis on competition and adverserialism, materialism and consumerism, individualism, a tendency to think and behave in fragmented ways, and the misuse of power. Concepts central to the integrative processes unfolding in the world include the oneness of all of creation, and the importance of unity in diversity. As these integrative processes unfold, key concepts are reconceptualised, including human rights, power and authority, justice, knowledge generation, consultation, scientific and spiritual enquiry, and the concept of religion itself.

The understanding of humanity's potential and destiny and the vision for humanity's future is, in light of the above, a positive one. The realization of that potential requires engagement on the part of the individuals, communities and institutions of society with the specific guidance, or divine plan, provided for this period of humanity's history.

# The Eternal Covenant

The relationship between the Creator and human beings takes the form of a covenant or agreement. God assures humanity that, out of His love, He will not abandon us. Rather, periodically, He will send His Messengers to guide humanity. Human beings, to uphold their part of the agreement, are to recognize His Messengers and be obedient to the divine laws revealed through Them.

In recent times the Manifestations of God, Adam, Krishna, Abraham, Moses, Buddha, Jesus, Muhammad, and now the Báb and Bahá'u'lláh, have fulfilled the Creator's promise.

> This is the changeless Faith of God, eternal in the past, eternal in the future.[124]

Our role now, is to recognize the spiritual truths of the teachings for this age, and apply them for the betterment of humanity.

> Abraham, on Him be peace, made a covenant concerning Moses and gave the glad-tidings of His coming. Moses made a covenant concerning the promised Christ, and announced the good news of His advent to the world. Christ made a covenant concerning the Paraclete and gave the tidings of His coming. The Prophet Muhammad made a covenant concerning the Báb, and the Báb was the One promised by Muhammad, for Muhammad gave the tidings of His coming. The Báb made a Covenant concerning the Blessed Beauty, Bahá'u'lláh, and gave the glad-tidings of His coming for the Blessed Beauty was the One promised by the Báb. Bahá'u'lláh made a covenant concerning a Promised One Who will become manifest after one thousand or thousands of years.[125]

The culmination of this millennia-long process, of the progressive unfoldment of God's Will for humanity, is the guidance for this stage in the collective development of the human race, revealed by Bahá'u'lláh.

> The Revelation identified with Bahá'u'lláh abrogates unconditionally all the Dispensations gone before it, upholds uncompromisingly the eternal verities they enshrine, recognizes firmly and absolutely the Divine origin of their Authors, preserves inviolate the sanctity of their authentic Scriptures, disclaims any intention of lowering the status of their Founders or of abating the spiritual ideals they inculcate, clarifies and correlates their functions, reaffirms their common, their unchangeable and fundamental purpose, reconciles their seemingly divergent claims and doctrines, readily and gratefully recognizes their respective contributions to the gradual unfoldment of one Divine Revelation, unhesitatingly acknowledges itself to be but one link in the chain of continually progressive Revelations, supplements their teachings with such laws and ordinances as conform to the imperative needs, and are dictated by the growing receptivity, of a fast evolving and constantly changing society, and proclaims its readiness and ability to fuse and incorporate the contending sects and factions into which they have fallen into a universal Fellowship, functioning within the framework, and in accordance with the precepts, of a divinely conceived, a world-unifying, a world-redeeming Order.[126]

In addition to the Eternal Covenant of God, described above, and to prevent the fragmentation that occurred on the passing of the Manifestation of God in each of the dispensations of the past, Bahá'u'lláh has provided the Lesser Covenant.

# The Lesser Covenant

The Covenant made by Bahá'u'lláh with His followers concerning His immediate successor is known as the Lesser Covenant. "Never before has a Manifestation of God left behind an authoritative statement in which He has explicitly directed His people to turn to someone as His successor, or follow a defined system of administration for governing the religious affairs of the community."[127] Bahá'u'lláh instructed His followers to turn to His eldest Son 'Abdu'l-Bahá, appointing Him as the Center of His Covenant.

Upon the passing of 'Abdu'l-Bahá, the followers of Bahá'u'lláh were directed to turn to the Administrative Order of Bahá'u'lláh, headed by an appointed guardian and an elected body known as the Universal House of Justice. 'Abdu'l-Bahá's grandson, Shoghi Effendi, served as the first and only guardian.

> The Unifier and Redeemer of all mankind, has proclaimed the advent of God's Kingdom on earth, has formulated its laws and ordinances, enunciated its principles, and ordained its institutions. To direct and canalize the forces released by His Revelation He instituted His Covenant, whose power has preserved the integrity of His Faith, maintained its unity and stimulated its worldwide expansion throughout the successive ministries of 'Abdu'l-Bahá and Shoghi Effendi.[128]

The Guardian, Shoghi Effendi, passed away in 1957. He did not appoint a successor and the line of guardians thus ceased. In 1963 the central elected institution of the Lesser Covenant, the Universal House of Justice was elected for the first time. It comprises nine individuals elected from any nation of the world. The Universal House of Justice continues to be elected every five years. It is an institution ordained by Bahá'u'lláh Himself and, though the individual members have no special status, as a body the Universal House of Justice is infallibly guided.

Seat of the Universal House of Justice — Bahá'í Arc, Mt. Carmel, Haifa, Israel.

# Universal House of Justice

Today, firmness in the Covenant of God is dependent on acceptance of the divine authority of, and obedience to the Universal House of Justice. Obedience to the Universal House of Justice allows humanity to align its will with Divine Will and Purpose, to ensure the harmonious and continuous operation of the forces delivered by Bahá'u'lláh's Revelation, and to build the social foundation of oneness from which a divine civilization will emerge.

> Unto the Most Holy Book every one must turn, and all that is not expressly recorded therein must be referred to the Universal House of Justice. That which this body, whether unanimously or by a majority doth carry, that is verily the truth and the purpose of God Himself. Whoso doth deviate therefrom is verily of them that love discord, hath shown forth malice, and turned away from the Lord of the Covenant.[129]

The Administrative Order of the Bahá'í Faith is fundamentally different from anything that any Manifestation of God has previously established, inasmuch as Bahá'u'lláh has Himself revealed its principles, established its institutions, appointed His successors to interpret His Word, and conferred the necessary authority on the Universal House of Justice which is designed to supplement and apply His legislative ordinances.[130]

> For Bahá'u'lláh, we should readily recognize, has not only imbued mankind with a new and regenerating Spirit. He has not merely enunciated certain universal principles, or propounded a particular philosophy, however potent, sound and universal these may be. In addition to these He, as well as 'Abdu'l-Bahá after Him, has, unlike the Dispensations of the past, clearly and specifically laid down a set of Laws, established definite institutions, and provided for the essentials of a Divine Economy. These are destined to be a pattern for future society, a supreme instrument for the establishment of the Most Great Peace, and the one agency for the unification of the world, and the proclamation of the reign of righteousness and justice upon the earth.[131]

Terraces of the Bahá'í Faith around the Shrine of the Báb — Mount Carmel, Haifa, Israel.

Through the Universal House of Justice and the innumerable efforts of devotees to Bahá'u'lláh, a Divine Order will be made manifest in the world of humanity.

> The Spirit breathed by Bahá'u'lláh upon the world … can never permeate and exercise an abiding influence upon mankind unless and until it incarnates itself in a visible Order, which would bear His name, wholly identify itself with His principles, and function in conformity with His laws.[132]

The unchallengeable authority and assurance of divine guidance conferred upon the Universal House of Justice in the sacred Scriptures make it, at this time, the supreme and central institution of the Faith to which all must turn. The world can have complete confidence in the ability of the Universal House of Justice to function under the unerring guidance of God.

The advancement of humanity towards its destined mature state is guided by the Universal House of Justice. Steps in the process take the form of successive plans initiated by that body. These plans originate in a charter revealed by 'Abdu'l-Bahá in 1916-17, referred to as The Tablets of the Divine Plan.

At the same time as the Bahá'í communities and like-minded friends are consciously applying the healing medicine of Baha'u'llah's teachings to an ailing humanity through a series of plans guided by the Universal House of Justice, the integrative forces are also manifesting themselves in various ways in the world at large, though the Source of change is not acknowledged.

The world, unaware of the Revelation of Bahá'u'lláh, is working its way toward the Lesser Peace - a political unification of the planet. The Lesser Peace will be followed by the Most Great Peace - a deeper, lasting expression of the oneness of humanity and all of creation, dependent on the conscious recognition of the Revelation of Bahá'u'lláh.

# The Lesser Peace & The Most Great Peace

The Lesser Peace within the world will be a political unity arrived at by governments of the world. This unity of nations will arise from a recognition that the peoples of all nations, are members of one common human family. This stage will not be reached as a result of direct action of the Bahá'í community.[133]

> Bahá'ís do not believe the transformation thus envisioned will come about exclusively through their own efforts. Nor are they trying to create a movement that would seek to impose on society their vision of the future. Every nation and every group—indeed, every individual—will, to a greater or lesser degree, contribute to the emergence of the world civilization towards which humanity is irresistibly moving. Unity will progressively be achieved, as foreshadowed by 'Abdu'l-Bahá, in different realms of social existence, for instance, "unity in the political realm", "unity of thought in world undertakings", "unity of races" and the "unity of nations". As these come to be realized, the structures of a politically united world, which respects the full diversity of culture and provides channels for the expression of dignity and honor, will gradually take shape.[134]

However, this does not imply that Bahá'í community is passively waiting for peace:

> ...by promoting the principles of the Faith, which are indispensable to the maintenance of peace, and by fashioning the instruments of the Bahá'í Administrative Order, ...the Bahá'ís are constantly engaged in laying the groundwork for a permanent peace, ...[135]

The Lesser Peace is but a stage in a process leading to the Most Great Peace. The Most Great Peace will be:

> ...a practical consequence of the spiritualization of the world and the fusion of all its races, creeds, classes and nations—can rest on no other basis, and can be preserved through no other agency, except the divinely appointed ordinances that are implicit in the World Order that stands associated with His Holy Name.[136]

# Reflections on the Life of the Spirit

Ruhi Institute

Book 1

# Ruhi Institute

The Ruhi Institute is an educational institution located in Colombia, South America. It generates materials, the purpose of which is the development of human resources with the qualities, attitudes, capabilities, and skills to contribute to spiritual, social, and cultural development. Its materials, which have emerged from a consistent effort to apply Bahá'í principles to the analysis of social conditions, have proven effective in diverse contexts worldwide.

The Ruhi Institute seeks to contribute to transformation of human society through engagement with two parallel processes: "the transformation of the individual, and the deliberate creation of the structures of a new society".[137] It fosters change in mental, cultural, scientific and technological, educational, economic and social structures.

> The Ruhi Institute directs its present efforts to develop human resources within a set of activities that conduce to spiritual and intellectual growth, but are carried out in the context of each individual's contribution to the establishment of new structures, whether in villages and rural regions or in large urban centers.[138]

A central principle and goal of the Ruhi Institute is universal participation. The courses of the Institute combine classroom learning and personal study with acts of service in the community. These courses seek to release the potential in each human being to direct their energies towards promoting the well-being of the community, with a vision of a new world civilization which will "embody in all its structures and processes the fundamental principle of the unity of the human race".[139]

As the nobility of the human being is central to the design and implementation of educational activities of the Institute, education, is not simply seen as "the acquisition of knowledge and the development of skills".[140] Rather true education constitutes the development of "vast and powerful potentialities inherent in the very nature of every human being".[141] The development of these potentialities and talents, "attains fruition when it is pursued in the spirit of service to humanity and in the context of creating a new world civilization".[142]

Each participant in the programs of the Ruhi Institute acts as a student in certain educational activities, and as a tutor in others. The institute, then, uses the term "collaborator" to refer to all who take part in its programs. Based on the conditions and the needs of the population served by the institute, courses are designed along a series of "paths of service" which a collaborator follows according to personal interests and capacities. At the beginning of each path of service collaborators mostly learn and develop new concepts and skills. Later on, they participate in courses that prepare them to act as tutors of the earlier courses, thus creating a unique and dynamic environment for the development of human resources.[143]

Some of the outcomes of the Ruhi Institute courses include the fostering of communities characterized by:

…an emerging pattern of devotional life in which people from all religious traditions and backgrounds are drawing spiritual sustenance, together from the same Divine Source.[144]

…a growing commitment to the spiritual education of children, so that the consciousness of the oneness of humanity, and the spiritual insights and qualities that are requisites of oneness, take firm root in the minds and hearts of the next generation.[145]

…a growing dedication to the spiritual empowerment of junior youth, who are learning how to channel their energies towards constructive ends within a framework of oneness.[146]

[a commitment to] learning how to systematically train growing numbers of youth and adults to become agents of community transformation by tending to the spiritual foundations of community life…[147]

These communities then, are building capacity to:

…engage in increasingly complex forms of social action that contribute to the improvement of their material conditions, so that their spiritual and material advancement can proceed in a coherent manner. And such communities are, in the process, learning how to draw on the insights and experiences they are gaining in all of these ways to contribute to the evolution of social thought within the arena of public discourse.[148]

Sharing book cover — design by David Peters for the Wikimedia Foundation.

# An Invitation

The community building processes inspired by the teachings of Bahá'u'lláh, are unfolding in every country of the world. The Ruhi Institute courses are available in every region of the world. These processes do not seek commitment to a set of static and outdated beliefs and practices. They seek the engagement of all in the transformation of the individuals, communities and institutions of society and the release of human potential in service to the wellbeing of the whole human race.

Thus for a person of any age, in any location, wishing to participate in the transformation of themselves and their society, there are clear avenues and opportunities for engagement.

Blessings, both spiritual and material, await all individuals of insight who step forward into the realm of service for the betterment of humanity.

> … your desire to partake actively of the dangers and mysteries afflicting so many millions of people today, is natural, and a noble impulse, there can be no comparison between the value of Bahá'í work and any other form of service to humanity. If the Bahá'ís could evaluate their work properly they would see that whereas other forms of relief work are superficial in character, alleviating the sufferings and ills of men for a short time at best, the work they are doing is to lay the foundation of a new spiritual Order in the world founded on the Word of God, operating according to the laws He has laid down for this age. No one else can do this work except those who have fully realized the meaning of the Message of Bahá'u'lláh, whereas almost any courageous, sincere person can engage in relief work, etc. The believers are building a refuge for mankind. This their supreme sacred task and they should devote every moment they can to this task.[149]

> Immerse yourselves in the ocean of My words, that ye may unravel its secrets, and discover all the pearls of wisdom that lie hid in its depths. Take heed that ye do not vacillate in your determination to embrace the truth of this Cause — a Cause through which the potentialities of the might of God have been revealed, and His sovereignty established. With faces beaming with joy, hasten ye unto Him. This is the changeless Faith of God, eternal in the past, eternal in the future. Let him that seeketh, attain it; and as to him that hath refused to seek it — verily, God is Self-Sufficient, above any need of His creatures.[150]

# Michelangela

**website** - www.michelangela.com.au
**email** - info@michelangela.com.au

To receive Michelangela's occasional
product announcements
please visit our website to subscribe.

# Unity in Diversity

This brightly illustrated picture book contains five simple stories for young readers. They foster an understanding of the oneness of the human race and celebrate its diversity within that unity.

Likening the human race to various colored cotton in a woven cloth, various fruits on the tree of life, stars in the heavens, members of one body, and different notes in one perfect chord, the stories use the concrete to teach the abstract.

Young readers will enjoy the bright colors and simple text as they develop their understanding of the unity and diversity of the human race.

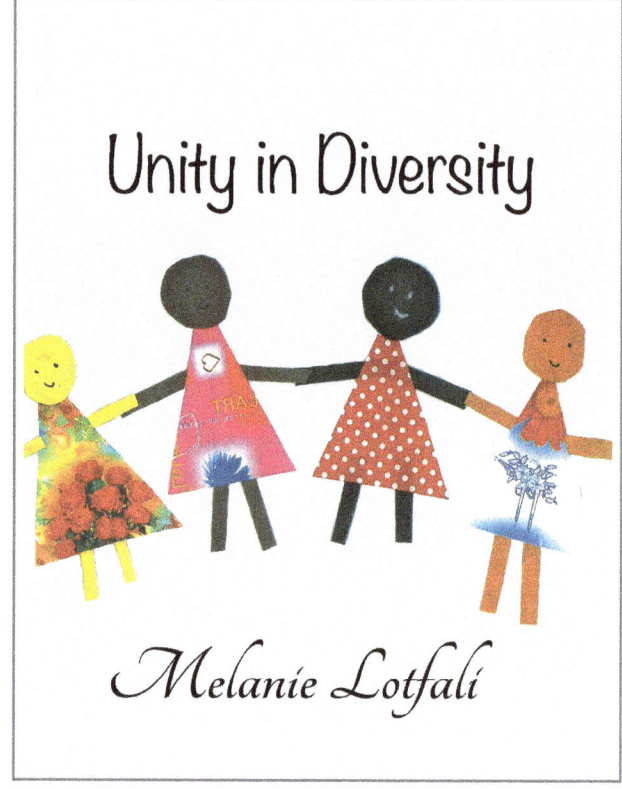

Ideal for children aged 4-8 years.

Order online from print-on-demand services, and digitally from the iBookstore. Also available as read-to-me stories in English, from the iBookstore.

Translated into French, Portuguese, Romanian, Tetum, and Mongolian.

# Fellowship Farm

Leezah, Skye-Maree and Olingah Fitzgerald live with their parents on Fellowship Farm. In the first book of the *Fellowship Farm* series, you will meet the children and learn about their daily activities on the farm.

There is a lot to be done each day: pillow fights, morning prayers, pig feeding and school bus riding. They help their dad feed the cows, add stickers to their virtues poster and learn to deal with bullies.

Then you will join the Fitzgerald children on their many adventures with puppies, snake bites, treasure hunts, bonfires, camping by the sea, and tree houses. And as they go they sometimes practice their virtues, and sometimes forget…

Five volumes in the series, covering books 1-15.

Suitable for independent readers aged 8-12 years; parent-read from six years.

Order online from print-on-demand services, and digitally from the iBookstore or Kindle store.

# The Big Story

This is the first book in the *Reflections on Reality* series.

*The Big Story* explains the way in which the divinely ordained and guided process that has brought human beings into existence has taken place gradually over time and space. It shows that the concepts of evolution and creation are not mutually exclusive.

Science and religion are shown to be two windows on one reality, two knowledge systems that when properly understood, function as one cohesive whole.

Suitable for independent readers aged 14+ years; with assistance from 12+.

Order online from print-on-demand services, and digitally from the iBookstore.

# Crowned Heart

The *Crowned Heart* series is the popular and inspiring collection of stories for young readers, drawn from Lights of Fortitude. It introduces three beloved heroines of the Faith.

"How many queens of the world have laid down their heads on a pillow of dust and disappeared... Not so the handmaids who ministered at the Threshold of God; these have shone forth like glittering stars in the skies of ancient glory, shedding their splendors across all the reaches of time." - `Abdu'l-Bahá.

These are the stories of Hand of the Cause of God, Martha Root, Clara Dunn and Corrine True. These easy to read stories are accompanied by truly exquisite watercolor illustrations by Katayoun Mottahedin.

Enjoyable reading for children 4-8 years of age.

Order online from print-on-demand services, and digitally from the iBookstore.

# Dr Melanie Lotfali

Author of the *Fellowship Farm* series, *Crowned Heart* series, and *Unity in Diversity* series.

Melanie Lotfali PhD is a graduate of the Australian College of Journalism in Professional Writing for Children. She is the author of twenty plus-books of fiction and non-fiction for children, and the illustrator of five.

Melanie has taught spiritual education classes for children for the past twenty years in five countries and is currently an active animator and trainer of animators for the Junior Youth Spiritual Empowerment Program. She is a qualified counselor and classroom teacher, and for the past six years has facilitated violence prevention and respectful relationships programs in high schools.

Much of her childhood was spent on the farms, beaches, and mountains of Tasmania, where the Fellowship Farm series is set. As an adult, she spent four years in Siberia and four years in East Timor as a pioneer.

She currently lives in Lismore, Australia, with her family.

# Michael Cohen

Author of the *Reflections on Reality* series and publisher of Michelangela's books.

Michael Cohen graduated as a Computer Systems Engineer in 1990 and worked for many years in software design and information systems. He changed careers in 2008 to become a Registered Nurse working in the area of Mental Health and Alcohol & Other Drugs.

Michael has been a keen participant in and advocate of the programs offered by The Foundation for the Application and Teaching of the Sciences (FUNDAEC) and Institute for Studies in Global Prosperity (ISGP).

He strives to contribute to processes and discourses leading to the progress of humankind toward a world society characterized by unity, justice and equity. A fundamental premise of Michael's worldview is that true science and true religion are necessarily in harmony, indeed are two windows on one reality. His writing seeks to promote understanding of this liberating concept and to contribute to a civilization that is ever advancing materially and spiritually.

He currently lives in Lismore, Australia, with his family.

# Image Bibliography

Cover - Crab Nebula © Space Telescope Science Institute - www.hubblesite.org
p06   Flower - pexels.com
p08   Holy Book - stock photo
p10   Progressive Revelation
p12   One Light many Lamps
p14   Sistine Chapel - BriYYZ (Flickr), Wikimedia Commons
p16   Hindu ritual
p18   Cenotaph of Abraham - محمد الفلسطيني, Wikimedia Commons
p20   Jewish Confirmation, Wikimedia Commons
p22   Zoroastrian Eternal Flame - Adam Jones, Wikimedia Commons
p24   Tibetan mandala - Wikimedia Commons
p26   Monks - pexels.com
p28   Christian Timkat ceremony - Jean Rebiffé, Wikimedia Commons
p30   Islamic Hajj - Al Jazeera English, Wikimedia Commons
p32   Astrolabe - Persian language Wikipedia
p34   Greatest Name Symbol - Sean Scully, Wikimedia Commons
p36   'Abdu'l-Bahá - Wikimedia commons
p38   Nuclear testing - United States Department of Defense, Wikimedia Commons
p40   Winter - pexels.com
p42   Fighting Hartebeest - Filip Lachowski, Wikimedia Commons
p44   American Football - Joe Bielawa, Wikimedia Commons
p46   Sale - Jonathan McIntosh, Wikimedia Commons
p48   Selfie - Biser Todorov, Wikimedia Commons
p50   Berlin Wall mural - Peter Rimar, Wikimedia Commons
p52   Concentration camp - Arnold E. Samuelson, Wikimedia Commons
p54   Earth - NASA, Wikimedia Commons
p56   Neurons - stock photo
p58   Paenibacillus vortex bacteria - Eshel Ben-Jacob, Wikimedia Commons
p60   Tulips - Ian Sane, Wikimedia Commons
p62   Isfahan Lotfollah mosque - Phillip Maiwald, Wikimedia Commons
p64   St Peter's Basilica - Becks, Wikimedia Commons
p66   Oblation statue - Wikimedia Commons
p68   United Nations General Assembly Hall - Basil Soufi, Wikimedia Commons
p80   Mandelbrot - Wikimedia Commons
p72   Justice Statue - Abolhassan Sadighi, Wikimedia Commons
p74   Wikimedia monument - Nostrix, Wikimedia Commons
p76   Wikimania 2012 - Helpameaout, Wikimedia Commons
p78   Consultation - stock photo
p82   Body of Knowledge, Jaume Plensa - Dontworry, Wikimedia Commons
p86   St Andrews Catholic Church - Joe Ravi, Wikimedia Commons
p90   Flower - pexels.com
p92   Holding Hands - pexels.com
p96   Universal House of Justice - Tom Habibi, Wikimedia Commons
p98   Shrine of the Báb - Danny Lyulyev, Wikimedia Commons
p102 Ruhi book 1 - Ruhi Institute
p104 World Flags - Wikimedia Commons
p106 Wiki Globe, Peter Davids - Jay Walsh, Wikimedia Commons

# References

1 Institute for Studies in Global Prosperity, 2014, Discourse and Social Transformation: Achieving Coherence, p71, unpublished
2 Gail M, 1953, Six Lessons on Islam, p1
3 'Abdu'l-Bahá, 1979, Foundations of World Unity, p15
4 Ibid.
5 'Abdu'l-Bahá, 1976, Bahá'í World Faith, p226
6 Bahá'u'lláh, 1857, The Hidden Words,
   http://www.bahai.org/library/authoritative-texts/bahaullah/hidden-words/
7 Bhagavad Gita, 4:7-8
8 Book of Genesis, 26:4
9 Kaaba - most holy place and site of pilgrimage for Moslems, Qur'an **2:125-127**
   http://quran.com/2/125-127
10 Deuteronomy 18:15, 18
11 https://en.wikipedia.org/wiki/Zoroaster
12 https://en.wikipedia.org/wiki/Zoroaster
13 Unknown origin
14 Digha-nikaya, IV.26
15 John 13:34
16 Gombrich E.H, 2005, A Little History of the World, p102
17 John 16:7
18 John 16:12-13
19 Abdul'baha, 1908, Some Answered Questions,
   http://www.bahai.org/library/authoritative-texts/abdul-baha/some-answered-questions/
20 Cobb S, 1963, Islamic Contributions to Civilization,
   http://bahai-library.com/cobb_islamic_contributions_civilization
21 Bahá'u'lláh, 1978, Proclamation of Bahá'u'lláh, p118
22 Shoghi Effendi, 1938, The Advent of Divine Justice, p72
   http://www.bahai.org/library/authoritative-texts/shoghi-effendi/advent-divine-justice/
23 Ibid.
24 Universal House of Justice, 2015, Riḍván 2015,
   http://www.bahai.org/library/authoritative-texts/the-universal-house-of-justice/messages/#d=20150421_001&f=f1
25 'Abdu'l-Bahá, 1912, The Promulgation of Universal Peace,
   http://www.bahai.org/library/authoritative-texts/abdul-baha/promulgation-universal-peace/
26 Karlberg M, 2014, Beyond a Culture of Contest, p48
27 Ibid., p40
28 Ibid., p41
29 The Prosperity of Humankind, Bahá'í International Community, 1995,
   https://www.bic.org/statements/prosperity-humankind#GU6OXfLqWoOM3Puk.97
30 Ruhi Institute, The Covenant of Bahá'u'lláh, Section 1.10
31 http://www.dictionary.com/browse/materialism?s=t
32 https://en.wikipedia.org/wiki/Materialism
33 Oxford Dictionary, http://www.oxforddictionaries.com/definition/english/materialism
34 https://en.wikipedia.org/wiki/Consumerism
35 Institute for Studies in Global Prosperity, 2014, Discourse and Social Transformation: Achieving Coherence, p127, unpublished
36 Ibid.
37 Bahá'u'lláh, The Kitáb-i-Iqan, p29
38 FUNDAEC, 2014, Constructing a Conceptual Framework for Social Action, p12, unpublished

39 http://www.oxforddictionaries.com/definition/english/power
40 Karlberg M, 2014, Beyond a Culture of Contest, p?
41 Universal House of Justice, 2013. Extracts written on behalf of the Universal House of Justice on the Subject of Chastity
   http://www.bahai.org/beliefs/life-spirit/character-conduct/articles-resources/selected-letters-subject-chastity
42 Bahá'u'lláh, 1891, Epistle to the Son of the Wolf
   http://www.bahai.org/library/authoritative-texts/bahaullah/epistle-son-wolf/#f=f2-3
43 Bahá'u'lláh, 1990, Gleanings From the Writings of Bahá'u'lláh, p260
   http://reference.bahai.org/en/t/b/GWB/gwb-122.html
44 Institute for Studies in Global Prosperity, 2014, Discourse and Social Transformation: Achieving Coherence, p87, unpublished
45 Universal House of Justice, 1995, Prosperity of Humankind,
   http://www.bahai.org/documents/bic-opi/prosperity-humankind
46 Institute for Studies in Global Prosperity, 2014, Discourse and Social Transformation: Achieving Coherence, p127, unpublished
47 Ibid., p87
48 Shoghi Effendi, 1941, The Promised Day Is Come,
   http://www.bahai.org/library/authoritative-texts/shoghi-effendi/promised-day-come/#f=f5-334
49 Institute for Studies in Global Prosperity, 2014, Discourse and Social Transformation: Achieving Coherence, p127, unpublished
50 Bahá'í International Community, 1995, The Prosperity of Humankind,
   http://www.bahai.org/library/other-literature/official-statements-commentaries/prosperity-humankind/#r=prh_en-title
51 Institute for Studies in Global Prosperity, 2014, Discourse and Social Transformation: Achieving Coherence, p87, unpublished
52 Ibid., p88
53 Ibid., p120
54 Ibid., p94
55 Shoghi Effendi, 1938, The World Order of Bahá'u'lláh: The Goal of a New World Order
   http://www.bahai.org/library/authoritative-texts/shoghi-effendi/world-order-bahaullah/#f=f4-111
56 Shoghi Effendi, 1938, The World Order of Bahá'u'lláh: The Goal of a New World Order
   http://www.bahai.org/library/authoritative-texts/shoghi-effendi/world-order-bahaullah/#f=f4-111
57 Bahá'u'lláh, 1873, The Kitáb-i-Aqdas
   http://www.bahai.org/library/authoritative-texts/bahaullah/kitab-i-aqdas/#f=f3-38
58 Institute for Studies in Global Prosperity, 2014, Discourse and Social Transformation: Achieving Coherence, p73, unpublished
59 Bahá'í International Community, 1995, The Prosperity of Humankind,
   http://www.bahai.org/library/other-literature/official-statements-commentaries/prosperity-humankind/#r=prh_en-title
60 'Abdu'l-Bahá, 1912, The Promulgation of Universal Peace,
   http://www.bahai.org/library/authoritative-texts/abdul-baha/promulgation-universal-peace/
61 Research Department of the Bahá'í World Centre, 2007, Ḥuqúqu'lláh - The Right of God, p7
62 Wikipedia, https://en.wikipedia.org/wiki/Human_rights
63 Weinberg M, 1996, The Human Rights Discourse: A Bahá'í Perspective, The Bahá'í World: 1996–97, p256–58.
64 Ibid., p248–50.
65 Bahá'í International Community, 1947, A Bahá'í Declaration of Human Obligations and Rights
66 Weinberg M, 1998, The Human Rights Discourse: A Bahá'í Perspective, The Bahá'í World: 1996–97, p248–50.
67 Ibid.
68 Universal House of Justice, Individual Rights and Freedoms,
   http://www.bahai.org/documents/the-universal-house-of-justice/individual-rights-freedoms
69 Institute for Studies in Global Prosperity, 2010, May Knowledge Grow in our Hearts, p70
   http://www.globalprosperity.org/documents/
   ISGP_May_Knowledge_Grow_in_our_Hearts_Applying_Spiritual_Principles_to_Development_Practice.pdf
70 Institute for Studies in Global Prosperity, 2014, Discourse and Social Transformation: Achieving Coherence, p115, unpublished
71 Ibid., p120
72 Ibid., p123
73 Ibid., p123
74 Ibid., p123
75 Universal House of Justice, 2013, To the Bahá'ís of Iran
   http://www.bahai.org/documents/the-universal-house-of-justice/bahais-iran-20130302_001
76 Bahá'í International Community, 1995, The Prosperity of Humankind,
   http://www.bahai.org/library/other-literature/official-statements-commentaries/prosperity-humankind/#r=prh_en-title
77 Bahá'u'lláh, Bishárát (Glad-Tidings), Tablets of Bahá'u'lláh revealed after the Kitáb-i-Aqdas,
   http://www.bahai.org/library/authoritative-texts/bahaullah/tablets-bahaullah/#f=f2-103

78 Institute for Studies in Global Prosperity, 2014, Discourse and Social Transformation: Achieving Coherence, p104, unpublished
79 Bahá'u'lláh, Kalimát-i-Firdawsíyyih (Words of Paradise), Tablets of Bahá'u'lláh revealed after the Kitáb-i-Aqdas,
    http://www.bahai.org/library/authoritative-texts/bahaullah/tablets-bahaullah/#r=tb_en-6
80 Institute for Studies in Global Prosperity, 2014, Discourse and Social Transformation: Achieving Coherence, p110, unpublished
81 The Prosperity of Humankind, Bahá'í International Community, 1995,
    https://www.bic.org/statements/prosperity-humankind#GU6OXfLqWoOM3Puk.97
82 Institute for Studies in Global Prosperity, 2014, Discourse and Social Transformation: Achieving Coherence, p89, unpublished
83 Ibid., p135
84 Universal House of Justice, 1995, Compilation on scholarship,
    http://reference.bahai.org/en/t/c/SCH/
85 Institute for Studies in Global Prosperity, 2014, Discourse and Social Transformation: Achieving Coherence, p135, unpublished
86 Universal House of Justice, 2010, Ridván 2010
    http://www.bahai.org/library/authoritative-texts/the-universal-house-of-justice/messages/#d=20100421_001&f=f1-35
87 Bahá'í International Community, 1995, The Prosperity of Humankind
    https://www.bic.org/statements/prosperity-humankind#yAScHcoRJ1GdFQJv.97
88 Bahá'u'lláh, Gleanings From the Writings of Bahá'u'lláh
    http://reference.bahai.org/en/t/b/GWB/gwb-81.html
89 'Abdu'l-Bahá, The Promulgation of Universal Peace
    http://reference.bahai.org/en/t/ab/PUP/pup-31.html
90 Bahá'u'lláh, 1995, The Prosperity of Humankind
    http://www.bahai.org/beliefs/universal-peace/articles-resources/consultation-quotes
91 Institute for Studies in Global Prosperity, 2014, Discourse and Social Transformation: Achieving Coherence, p133, unpublished
92 Bahá'u'lláh, 1998, Tablets of Bahá'u'lláh Revealed After the Kitáb-i-Aqdas, p168
93 'Abdu'l-Bahá, The Promulgation of Universal Peace
    http://reference.bahai.org/en/t/ab/PUP/pup-31.html
94 Institute for Studies in Global Prosperity, 2014, Discourse and Social Transformation: Achieving Coherence, p133, unpublished
95 'Abdu'l-Bahá, Selections From the Writings of 'Abdu'l-Bahá
    http://reference.bahai.org/en/t/ab/SAB/sab-44.html
96 'Abdu'l-Bahá, Star of the West, vol. 8, no. 9 (20 August 1917), p114
    http://bahai-library.com/compilation_consultation
97 'Abdu'l-Bahá, 1978, Selections from the Writings of 'Abdu'l-Bahá
    http://www.bahai.org/library/authoritative-texts/abdul-baha/selections-writings-abdul-baha/#f=f6-349
98 'Abdu'l-Bahá, Selections From the Writings of 'Abdu'l-Bahá
    http://reference.bahai.org/en/t/ab/SAB/sab-40.html
99 Bahá'í International Community, 1995, The Prosperity of Humankind,
    http://www.bahai.org/library/other-literature/official-statements-commentaries/prosperity-humankind/#f=f3-40
100 Institute for Studies in Global Prosperity, 2014, Discourse and Social Transformation: Achieving Coherence, p175, unpublished
101 Ibid., p130
102 Ibid., p72
103 Ibid., p117
104 'Abdu'l-Bahá , 1982, Promulgation of Universal Peace, p38
105 Institute for Studies in Global Prosperity, 2014, Discourse and Social Transformation: Achieving Coherence, 2015, p225, unpublished
106 Ibid., p73
107 Ibid., p72
108 Ibid., p171
109 Ibid., p131
110 Ibid., p131
111 Ibid., p130
112 Ibid., p117
113 https://en.wikipedia.org/wiki/Religion
114 'Abdu'l-Bahá, 1978, Selections from the Writings of 'Abdu'l-Bahá
    http://www.bahai.org/library/authoritative-texts/abdul-baha/selections-writings-abdul-baha/#f=f6-349
115 Universal House of Justice, 2002, To the World's Religious Leaders,
    http://www.bahai.org/library/authoritative-texts/the-universal-house-of-justice/messages/#d=20020401_001&f=f1-27
116 Bahá'u'lláh, Tablets of Bahá'u'lláh revealed after the Kitáb-i-Aqdas, p129
    http://www.bahai.org/library/authoritative-texts/bahaullah/tablets-bahaullah/#f=f4-338

117 Institute for Studies in Global Prosperity, 2014, Discourse and Social Transformation: Achieving Coherence, p220, unpublished
118 Ibid., p86
119 'Abdu'l-Bahá, 1875, The Secret of Divine Civilization
   http://www.bahai.org/library/authoritative-texts/abdul-baha/secret-divine-civilization/#f=f3-132
120 Institute for Studies in Global Prosperity, 2014, Discourse and Social Transformation: Achieving Coherence, p129
121 'Abdu'l-Bahá, 1912, The Promulgation of Universal Peace
   http://www.bahai.org/library/authoritative-texts/abdul-baha/promulgation-universal-peace/#f=f14-848
122 Bahá'u'lláh, Bahá'u'lláh and the New Era, 1980, p175
123 Institute for Studies in Global Prosperity, 2014, Discourse and Social Transformation: Achieving Coherence, p84, unpublished
124 Bahá'u'lláh, 1978, Proclamation of Bahá'u'lláh, p119
125 'Abdu'l-Bahá, 1976, Bahá'í World Faith - Selected Writings of Bahá'u'lláh and 'Abdu'l-Bahá, p358
126 Shoghi Effendi, 1944, God Passes By,
   http://www.bahai.org/library/authoritative-texts/shoghi-effendi/god-passes-by/#f=f8-177
127 http://covenantstudy.org/questions/lesser-covenant/
128 Universal House of Justice, 1972, The Constitution of the Universal House of Justice,
   http://www.bahai.org/documents/the-universal-house-of-justice/constitution-universal-house-justice
129 'Abdu'l-Bahá, 1922, Will and Testament of 'Abdu'l-Bahá
   http://www.bahai.org/library/authoritative-texts/abdul-baha/will-testament-abdul-baha/#f=f3-41
130 Shoghi Effendi, 1938, The World Order of Bahá'u'lláh
   http://www.bahai.org/library/authoritative-texts/shoghi-effendi/world-order-bahaullah/#r=wob_en-title
131 Ibid.
132 Ibid.
133 The Universal House of Justice Research Department, 1985, Peace
134 Universal House of Justice, 2013, To the Baha'is of Iran
   http://www.bahai.org/documents/the-universal-house-of-justice/bahais-iran-20130302_001
135 http://reference.bahai.org/en/t/c/CP/cp-75.html
136 http://www.bahai.org/library/authoritative-texts/shoghi-effendi/world-order-bahaullah/
137 http://www.ruhi.org/institute/index.php
138 Ibid.
139 Ibid.
140 Ibid.
141 Ibid.
142 Ibid.
143 Ibid.
144 Institute for Studies in Global Prosperity, 2014, Discourse and Social Transformation: Achieving Coherence, p97, unpublished
145 Ibid.
146 Ibid.
147 Ibid.
148 Ibid.
149 Shoghi Effendi, Lights of Guidance, p423
150 Bahá'u'lláh, 1992, The Kitáb-i-Aqdas, p85
   http://www.bahai.org/library/authoritative-texts/bahaullah/kitab-i-aqdas/#r=ka_en-title

www.ingramcontent.com/pod-product-compliance
Lightning Source LLC
Chambersburg PA
CBHW061935290426
44113CB00025B/2926